A FEAST OF FLAVOURS

A FEAST OF FLAVOURS

The New Vegetarian Cuisine

ANNIE BELL

BANTAM PRESS

LONDON · NEW YORK · TORONTO · SYDNEY · AUCKLAND

TRANSWORLD PUBLISHERS LTD
61-63 Uxbridge Road, London W5 5SA

TRANSWORLD PUBLISHERS (AUSTRALIA) PTY LTD
15-23 Helles Avenue, Moorebank, NSW 2170

TRANSWORLD PUBLISHERS (NZ) LTD
Cnr Moselle and Waipareira Aves,
Henderson, Auckland

Published 1992 by Bantam Press
a division of Transworld Publishers Ltd

A catalogue record for this book is
available from the British Library.

ISBN 0593 022149

Typeset in 11/13 pt Garamond by
Falcon Graphic Art Ltd,
Wallington, Surrey
Printed in Great Britain by
Mackays of Chatham Plc, Chatham, Kent.

For my husband Jonnie, and my son Rothko

Acknowledgements

I should like to thank the following people and companies for their specialist knowledge: Charles Carey of the Oil Merchant, Julian Birch of the South Bank Seafood Company, Chris Newnes and Robin Bruce of C.J. Newnes, Christopher Kerrison of the Colchester Oyster Fishery, Randolph Hodgson of Neal's Yard Dairy, Monika Lavery and Emma Ranson of Brindisa, Antonio Carluccio of the Neal Street Restaurant, M.J. Hyams Fruit and Vegetable Supplier, the French Garden in Covent Garden, the French Kitchen Shop in Westbourne Grove, and Elizabeth Bell for her encyclopaedic and practical knowledge of the vegetable garden.

I am also grateful to Clarissa Dickson-Wright for goading me into picking up a pen in the first place, and to my husband, for quelling his carnivorous instincts while I wrote this book. Thank you also to my editor, Georgina Morley, for her unwavering enthusiasm and support, and to my family and to Ambikha for keeping the show running during times of crisis.

Contents

SPRING

Roasted New Potatoes

British and Irish Cheeses with Assorted Biscuits

Chocolate and Almond Cake

Salad of Lamb's Lettuce, Asparagus and Quail's Eggs

Goat's Cheese and Leek Profiteroles,
   with a Red Pepper Sauce

Tomato and Potato Gratin

Iced Mango Parfait

Risotto Nero (risotto made with squid's ink, mussels and clams)

Stuffed Squid Braised with Broad Beans

Artichoke Hearts Sautéed with Rocquette

Peaches Baked on Brioche with Sabayon Sauce

Buckwheat Crêpes, Onions Braised in Sherry Vinegar,
   and Sour Cream

Gratin of Salmon with Sorrel Sauce

Warm Salad of Oyster Mushrooms and Saffron

Rhubarb Tart

SUMMER

Niçoise Platter

Potato Salad Ravigote

Mesclun Dressed with Lemon Juice and
   Extra Virgin Olive Oil

Sun-dried Tomato Bread

Fig Tart

Char-grilled Tuna Marinated with Garlic

Salad of Plum Tomatoes and Basil

Borlotti Beans with Radicchio
Spanish Omelette

Miniature Goat's Cheeses

Green Salad with Nasturtiums

Nest of Quail's Eggs

Salad of Roasted Peppers with Capers

Sweet and Sour Baby Onions

Salad of Broad Beans and Green Beans

Aubergine and Coriander Purée

Selection of Olives, Chillies and Sun-dried Tomatoes

Apricot, Almond and Chocolate Meringue

Ginger Cake

Basket of Summer Fruits

Selection of Crostini
    with Tapenade and Grilled Red Pepper
    with Aubergine Purée and Sun-dried Tomato
    with Ricotta, Crushed Basil and Pine-nuts

Platter of Salted Almonds, Cheese Bouchées, Olives,
    and Chillies on Rye

Char-grilled Vegetables with Romesco Sauce

Seafood Fritters

Exotic Fruits

AUTUMN

Red Pepper Stuffed with Green Herbs and
    Pine-Nuts, in a Tomato Mayonnaise

Orecchiette, Aubergine and Capers

WINTER

Introduction

In a day when everyone from the farmer to the man at the Ministry through to the buyer of a large supermarket is working all out to eradicate and ignore the seasons, seasonality is almost nostalgic. 'Flagship' supermarkets openly pursue a policy of year-round availability, stocking UK produce where possible, supplementing it with imports between times. This puts pressure on the farmer to compete with imports, and it is the job of the man at the Ministry to facilitate this by creating the right environment.

Even the harvest is not when it used to be; by the time the harvest moon is in the sky the crops have long since been gathered. Mild winters and early springs, helped along by methods of early pollination and the use of sprays to set the pollen, have put paid to the harvest festival as our grandparents knew it.

Seasonality of produce may be a thing of the past but no amount of artifice and chemistry can eradicate the seasons themselves. There will always be a prime time to eat produce, and nothing can remove the wealth of tradition surrounding food which has built up over the years, formulated by the seasons and all their attributes. The seasons not only offer timely produce but lend their mood to dishes too. These are traditions which will continue for as long as the seasons do.

In creating these menus, for each season, I looked first to produce in its prime and then to the different qualities of that season, so that the dishes truly represent the time of year. I also followed the instinct of my palate, which cried out for an antidote to the excesses of each season long before it had ended. The menus were assembled over the period of a year, as a natural progression of produce, mood, colours and atmosphere.

Should this book have appeared during the early 1980s it might, quite justifiably, have been criticized for relying on elusive ingredients. The food retail scene has changed so dramatically since then that anyone who, like me, relies for most goods on a large supermarket will be familiar with every ingredient in the book. The progressive improvement in the choice of fruit and vegetables available is, in part, a result of mistakes made in trying to steer agricultural production with subsidies. This created the absurd grain mountains and wine lakes of the late 1970s and early 1980s. It became essential for land to be taken out of surplus production and put to alternative uses, either to be managed or to be used to grow new varieties of crops. It has encouraged experimentation with less productive methods of farming using fewer fertilizers, such as organic farming.

We have a band of bright, enterprising producers to thank, too, who are prepared to test the market and take advantage of the aware consumer. Consumers today are interested in new foods; they are taste-conscious and variety-conscious. They may already have tried a dish abroad or eaten it in a restaurant. The supermarket acts as an agent, interpreting consumer demand and keeping in touch with producers. A buyer will visit a farm and, providing the grower can supply the necessary quantity of a commodity to the required standard at a marketable price, the supermarket will consider stocking it. It also provides leaflets to explain the use of unusual items.

'Try everything, keep that which is good' is a fine maxim to apply to food. Being innately curious about food, I always try new vegetables and fruit, or interesting-looking packages. Some are instantly binned, but others become new favourites and new ingredients to play with. Ingredients are like the colours in an artist's palette. This is particularly relevant to the modern-day vegetarian; there is vast scope for interesting, imaginative cooking making use of everything that is available. Taking new produce on board involves a process of re-education, but varieties that are unusual today will be commonplace tomorrow.

'In time, vegetarians lose their liking for preparations possessing much flavour and seasoning and usually prefer simple fare' — so wrote Mrs Beeton over 100 years ago. This vision of vegetarians as some alternative life-form has persisted until very recently. For years meatless food has attracted an appended apology. This is evident in the attempts made by so many food manufacturers to produce the meat-form using vegetarian ingredients — vegetarian cutlets, burgers, sausages and pâté all grace the grocer's shelf. To approach meatless food with any degree of success it is essential to shift the focus away from a central protein and redefine the structure of a meal. Within vegetarian cooking there is no equivalent to meat around which to centre a menu, at least, no palatable one. It is not even a dietary necessity. The belief for the best part of this century that everyone must eat about ½ lb of solid protein a day is a myth — in fact, around 2 oz a day is adequate. A vegetarian menu should be a harmonious balance of tastes and textures, proteins, vegetables, carbohydrates and fats.

'I'm a vegetarian, but I eat fish' seems to have taken a firm hold in English phraseology. It is a phrase I have heard more times than I can count. *Larousse Gastronomique* defines vegetarianism as 'A type of diet that totally excludes meat, poultry, and sometimes fish, but permits eggs, milk, cheese and sometimes butter.' There is no doubt that a sizeable proportion of those people who consider themselves to be vegetarian do include fish in their diet. One of the aims of this book is to look at vegetarianism in its broadest sense, which is why I have chosen to include fish. There is no moral foundation to this decision, and it is not by way of saying that a vegetarian diet ought to include fish. I have used fish more as an ingredient than in its traditional role as star of the show. In a number of instances, as indicated, it can be omitted from the dish.

Being none too fond of unrefined foods 'en masse', I use them only if they are of gastronomic benefit to the dish. Pastry is best made with white flour; wholemeal flour gives pastry a gritty texture that jars with the smoothness of a filling. Both wholegrain breads and those made with refined flour have a place on the dinner table. Pulses can be fabulous interrupted with a contrasting food, but without that interruption, or paired with an equally heavy food, they tend to be unpalatable and indigestible. A meal should leave you feeling satisfied, it should be pleasant to look at, and should please the palate; but it should not leave you uncomfortably aware of your stomach and tired.

The menus in this book are arranged seasonally and roughly divide into two types: buffet menus and those intended for a seated meal around a table, consisting of a number of small courses. These latter menus move away from the traditional approach of starter, main course and side dishes, followed by desserts and cheese. By removing the focus of the meal each menu is a progression of small courses that balance and mingle with each other. Each menu is a dietary balance of ingredients; it is simply a reinterpretation of a more traditional meal.

'Buffets de Gare' were established in France to cater to the needs of travellers on lengthy journeys. The advent of fast trains and on-train facilities diminished the role of the original establishments, just a few of which remain. A buffet as we know it today is a means of serving a large number of guests without the formal provisions of a seated dinner, which would turn it into a banquet. The practical requirements of a buffet place it at an immediate gastronomic disadvantage. It must be suitable for eating with fork in one hand, plate in the other — and a large number of dishes must be eaten simultaneously: potentially disastrous if the dishes rubbing shoulders on the plate should start to compete with each other. The buffet menus have been assimilated with an overall effect in mind, putting together a selection of dishes which blend well together and balance. There are no sequences to play with in a buffet. These menus have a versatility, though, and can be rearranged into courses for a seated meal if required.

Menus are given for hot and cold buffets. A cold buffet is an extremely useful card in entertaining. These menus tend to be centred around Mediterranean ingredients and flavours, which lend themselves with particular grace to this type of meal. The colours and strength of flavours carry well into cold food. 'Cold' is not to say refrigerated, unless specified. Cooked food to be served cold should be allowed to cool to room temperature and then served. Refrigerating dishes can remove the freshness, alter textures and kill flavours, although if it is unavoidable, then remove the food from the refrigerator and allow it to stand at room temperature for an hour before the meal.

Hot food should be served very hot on warm plates. Hot food partially chilled by a cold plate or inadequately hot in the first place can mean curtains for that dish.

To produce a whole menu will require time and forethought. I am not a disciple of the ten-minute feast. Arguably some of the best dishes are the simplest, but 'you get out what you put in' holds true for others. At the end of the day it should be a happy balance of the two. The recipes are earthy but elegant, they are relaxed in style and presentation, so the dishes are equally suitable as part of a simpler everyday meal. The food is highly versatile and will lend itself to any occasion — it is the occasion that should dictate the length of the meal and the progression of courses.

There are two extreme schools of thought on how much detail should be given in a recipe. Those like Marcel Boulestin believe that it is impossible to give exact recipes so refrain from giving almost any detail. Others give minute details of every step they have taken to arrive at a certain result. I am one of the 'others' in this respect, and I have given every detail I consider to be relevant to create the recipe. This is not to say that the recipes are complicated, or that you should not change or omit stages if you see fit. It is simply my version of events. One detail in which I shy away from giving specific amounts is the seasoning. In many instances this is a personal requirement. I like food to be well seasoned, but I know many people who do not. While I believe that there is a critical point for many dishes whereby the seasoning maximizes the flavours, it may not be the same for everyone.

Some of the recipes may be unfamiliar to you – I am always intrigued by the oddness of recipes. I like food which surprises me and challenges any preconceived notions I have, and I have found that unusual combinations of food often work well together.

None of the recipes is technically difficult. Thankfully we tend to be good at those things we enjoy doing – so provided you are enthusiastic and find pleasure in the preparation of a meal, you will cook well.

SPECIFICATIONS

Each recipe serves 6 people unless otherwise indicated; served as a main course, though, some of the dishes should be increased in quantity. All recipes were tested in a fan-assisted electric oven. Ovens do vary enormously, so keep a watchful eye on the first couple of recipes you try in case times and temperatures differ with the use of your own oven, and make a note of the variations.

Salt

Use fine-grain sea salt, or coarse-grain sea salt in a grinder.

Pepper

Unless otherwise stated, use freshly ground black pepper; produced from whole, dried red peppercorns, this is hot and aromatic. Other peppers used are freshly ground white pepper, which is less spicy and often more suitable with fish and in white sauces, and cayenne pepper, used when a touch of heat is desired.

Eggs

Use size 2 free-range eggs. Occasionally size 5 eggs are indicated. Store eggs pointed end down, in a cool place; to whip egg whites bring them back to room temperature. Once washed, eggs become pervious to odours, desirable should you be the fortunate guardian of a clutch of truffles, but as a general rule avoid washing them.

Eggs will keep for up to a month. They gradually lose moisture through their porous shell, becoming lighter as time progresses. The freshness of an egg can be tested by lowering it into heavily salinated water. If it sinks it is less than three days old. If it takes up a half-mast position it is between three and six days old, and if it floats it is decidedly old.

Breads

A number of the menus recommend particular breads to accompany the dishes. It is possible to buy an increasing number of speciality breads whose characteristics can be paired with a meal. After considerable research and experimentation I decided that the detail and knowledge required to bake bread at home was beyond the scope of this book.

Flour

Unless otherwise stated, use plain white flour.

Butter

Use unsalted or slightly salted butter. Where butter is used in its natural state, or plays a predominant role, seek out a good French unsalted butter.

Vinegars

Most of the vinaigrette recipes call for sherry vinegar, or a good red wine vinegar aged in oak. Keep a bottle of white wine vinegar to hand for acidulating water, for *beurres blancs* and for hollandaise sauces. For balsamic vinegar, see p. 157.

Arachide Oil

Also called peanut or groundnut oil, this is a neutral-tasting oil suitable for deep-frying or for use in combination with stronger oils.

Olive Oil

Olive oil has become a connoisseur's art during the last decade. I am immediately impressed by a wine merchant if I see shelves of estate-bottled olive oils alongside the shelves of wine. Most delicatessens will also stock some estate-bottled oils, and as I write they have just begun creeping on to the supermarket shelf. I owe my knowledge of this product to Charles Carey. During the early 1980s, through his company The Oil Merchant, he began importing estate-, farm- or village-produced extra virgin olive oil from Italy, France, Spain and Greece, and subsequently extended this to include the best commercial extra virgin and pure olive oils and other related products. Olive oil plays a major role in this book, and in vegetarian food generally. So much of the cuisine of the oil-producing countries is naturally vegetarian that it is worth looking to them for inspiration. This is an area of good food to which those who have been forced to relinquish fats in their diet, and are concerned about cholesterol, should turn.

The process of making olive oil starts during early November. The perfect olive oil would be produced in the following fashion. First the ripe olives are hand-picked from the trees. They are taken to the press the same day, before any fermenting can occur, though they may be slightly bruised. They are washed to remove any chemical residues, and leaves and twigs are removed. The olives are crushed to a paste between granite stones and spread on straw mats with a central hole, to a depth of about 2 inches. Often the straw mats are replaced by modern plastic mats. These mats are stacked some 6 feet high, then they are wheeled to a press and a perforated tube descends through the central hole in the mat. A hydraulic press slowly starts to apply pressure, and simultaneously warm water flows from the holes in the tube, washing the paste. The warmer the water the more oil will be extracted, though there is an optimum temperature for this pressing. The resulting liquid is a murky mixture of oil, water, and liquid from the olive. Traditionally the water is separated from the oil in a series of settling tanks, but because of the length of time this takes, the usual procedure now is to perform this task in a centrifuge. The resulting oil is called the first cold pressing. Occasionally house-style comes into play during the first pressing: some straw may be thrown in with the olives to give them a 'traditional' tone, or some lemons included to impart their natural oils to the finished product, or perhaps some leaves to deepen the colour. It is a myth, though, that the greener the oil the better its quality, as Ligurians, so proud of their pale oil, will tell you. The oil is now usually filtered through cotton gauze to render it crystal clear. Some producers bottle unrefined oil, which is slightly more pungent and peppery. The resulting pulp can be washed again, using higher pressure and hotter water to produce a little more oil, or it can be sold to a commercial refiner who, through various chemical processes and heating it to a high heat, will extract a tasteless refined oil.

Virgin oils have an acidity of less than 4 per cent, and extraction is purely a mechanical process. The finest of the categories within this group is extra virgin olive oil, which must have an acidity of less than 1 per cent. The lower the acidity, the greater the attention that will have been paid to the olives while they were growing and when they were harvested. If the olives start to ferment, either because they have been harvested late when they are black and greasy, or are infested, or have been left in a heap before pressing, then the acidity will start to rise. Oil with an acidity of more than 4 per cent cannot be sold for human consumption and must be refined. Commercially produced and blended oils need not state what proportion of different oils has been used; this applies to pure olive oils, a mixture of virgin olive oil and refined oil, and to extra virgin olive oil. Estate-produced and bottled extra virgin olive oil is a guarantee of what is in the bottle, which goes some way towards justifying the price. With pure olive oil, the only indicators of the proportion of virgin olive oil to refined oil are taste and price.

A practice specific to Italy is the blending of olive oil. Such is the demand for Italian olive oil, reputedly the best in the world, that they are unable to produce enough to meet either their internal or their export demand. Italy is the largest importer of olive oil as well as the largest exporter. Large commercial producers buy in oil from Greece and Spain and blend it to produce a standard quality of oil that will be acceptable to supermarkets. This is what is found on most supermarket shelves. It is legal to sell a bottle of olive oil in this country which says 'produce of Italy' on it, if it was blended or produced in Italy, but the oil need not be Italian, and a percentage probably is not.

Frosts in Tuscany in 1985, which killed many olive trees, resulted in a similar confusion for the consumer of estate-bottled oils. A number of estates which had established a market for their oils, and understandably did not wish to relinquish this, began buying in oil from other parts of Italy and blending it to be as close in style as their house oil used to be, changing the small print on the bottle to 'bottled by' as opposed to 'produced and bottled by'. Thankfully the olive groves of Tuscany are now recovering and this practice is on the decline.

The blending of the oils is an extremely sophisticated process. All oil deteriorates slowly, and some olives produce an oil which is mild and gently loses its flavour, while others produce an oil which is strong to begin with and loses its flavour later. So it is important to achieve a happy blend that will not be too strong at the beginning of the year but will still be tasty at the end of it. If you are an *aficionado* of olive oil, it is a good idea to buy in the new season's oil by February. It is quite strong and peppery to begin with, which is not to everyone's taste, but it mellows after a few months.

If the oil of different countries could be broadly categorized, leading characteristics might be summarized as follows. Greek oil tends to be quite heavy and pungent; it can be greasy, as the commercial producers tend to let the olives get over-ripe in order to extract more oil, but the quality suffers. Italian oils tend to be elegant with a peppery aftertaste. They should have a balance between this aftertaste and the initial delicate flavour. It is wrong to have a throat-rasping aftertaste, and equally wrong if it is all fruity foretaste (which tends to characterize supermarket oils). French oils are sweeter and more aromatic, and Spanish oils could be described as almost nutty. Oils of the quality of estate-produced and bottled oils differ from grove to grove, and the choice of oil is very much a question of personal taste.

As a broad rule of thumb, the oils should be used according to the culinary practices of their countries. In Italy, where oil is used raw, dribbled over bread, vegetables or pulses, it takes the form of a condiment. In France and Spain it is used more as a cooking medium. In a perfect world you would keep a bottle of French and Italian oil to hand, and a good pure olive oil such as Plagniol for deep-frying, mayonnaise and general cooking purposes.

Oil will keep indefinitely if stored in the correct conditions. The perfect place is the cellar, or simulated conditions. The arch enemy is light, which oxidizes the oil, though it does contain natural anti-oxidants that will preserve it if correctly stored.

Fish

Britain has habitually neglected the rich pickings of its surrounding waters. It is a very sad fact that the greater part of the high-quality fish caught in British waters disappears to the Continent, where it can fetch a higher price. This is a simple result of supply and demand, and were such fish more highly valued over here, fishmongers would thrive and we might have the opportunity to cook and experiment with the seafood that is usually found only on the restaurant menu. In part, ignorance is to blame, a heritage of ignorance; if a child does not learn how to use and prepare something during the years spent with its parents, which on the whole it does not in this country, and if the science is not taught in schools, then it is up to the fledgling adult to fumble through with an instruction manual, which is not always the most encouraging way to learn.

Supermarkets, in part to blame for pushing out the high-street shop, do not have the trained staff to offer a desirable service or range of fish. All in all it is a fairly grim picture, with little ray of hope for the future other than that enough people will be sufficiently interested and concerned with what fish they can buy and eat to create the necessary demand for good fishmongers to thrive. All the fish used in this book are relatively readily available from a high-street fishmonger. There are many more varieties of fish which merit cooking and eating, and I would recommend that anyone who does eat fish buys a good guide such as Alan Davidson's *Mediterranean Seafood* and *North Atlantic Seafood*, or Jane Grigson's *Fish Cookery*, and experiments with tempting yet unfamiliar offerings from the fishmonger's slab.

More and more exotic fish are appearing, often snapped up and prepared with delicious skill by ethnic communities. The preparation of such fish requires a requisite knowledge, and one would do well to procure a book on the subject if interested. A visit to Billingsgate or to the wholesale fish markets of Birmingham, Manchester or Glasgow reveals box upon box of beautiful gleaming fish with crystal clear eyes, taut with rigor. A few days later the eyes will cloud over and the flesh slacken. Ethnic customers, for whom shopping in a market-place is indigenous to their culture, increasingly make up the numbers of the buyers in such markets. This is a delicate situation for our markets, which under the charter of James I were not intended for such trade, and traders are not really equipped to deal with it. But these are free markets and anyone can buy there. The ideal solution, which hopefully will be instigated in the near future, would be for wholesale buyers and restaurateurs to buy from the market during the first few hours of trading, and then at 7.00 a.m., when they are finished, for the market to open to the small retail buyer. Traders understandably discourage the small buyer, and do not like to break boxes if it can be helped, which is prohibitive to the enthusiastic cook, so it would be a welcome move for a system which catered for the small buyer to be instigated.

TERMS

Pages can be written delineating culinary terms, and while they play an essential role in the professional kitchen, for the most part they are obsolete and confusing to the domestic cook. I have avoided the use of such terminology unless it is in general use and is much easier than describing the process itself.

Concassée *Concasser* is French for chopping or pounding. Tomato concassée is the skinned and seeded flesh of tomatoes, finely diced. It also refers to the ice used to line, for example, a plate of oysters.
Chiffonade To prepare a chiffonade of sorrel or basil, place several leaves on top of each other, roll them into a tight scroll, and cut across the scroll to give thin strips of the leaf.
Julienne This is food cut into thin squared strips. First the food is thinly sliced (a mandolin will assist here), then the slices are cut into thin strips 2-5 cm (1-2 in) long.

BASIC PREPARATIONS

Sweet Pastry

This is a particularly crisp, buttery pastry. It is difficult to roll, and I normally press it into the required tin and then allow it to rest in the refrigerator for an hour, or freeze it in this state. The liquid used to bind the pastry can be selected to complement the filling: orange juice, lemon or lime juice and a dash of brandy or *eau-de-vie* can be used.

This quantity will make enough for one large or two small tart tins.

8 oz/225 g flour	*2 egg yolks (size 5)*
3 oz/85 g sugar	*1 teaspoon brandy*
4½ oz/130 g butter	*orange juice to bind*

Place the flour and sugar together in the bowl of a food processor. Add the butter, cut into pieces, and process the mixture to the consistency of fine crumbs. Incorporate the egg yolks. Add the brandy and bring the dough together with orange juice. Either wrap the dough in cling-film and allow it to rest for 1 hour in the fridge, or press it into the tart tin and then rest it.

Puff Pastry

For me, puff pastry still involves a trip to the supermarket. Julia Child gives detailed instructions on making it in *Mastering the Art of French Cooking*.

Vegetable Stock

Use any of the following vegetables: onion, leeks, carrots, celery, fennel, celeriac, courgettes, aubergine and mushrooms. Avoid cauliflower, cabbages and turnips, which will impart an unpleasant flavour to the stock. Cube the vegetables, fairly small, and sweat them in some oil or butter for 10 minutes. Include some lentils, a couple of garlic cloves, and a *bouquet garni* or some tarragon, chervil and parsley. Cover the vegetables with water and season the stock with salt and white peppercorns. Bring to the boil, and simmer for 35-45 minutes. It may require skimming during the early stages. Strain the stock — the fat can be skimmed off once it is cool if required.

Fish Stock

In a large saucepan place 2 lb/0.9 kg of fresh fish trimmings (sole, plaice, or halibut), heads and bones, or shellfish, with ½ pint of white wine. Add water just to cover, and bring slowly to the boil. Skim the stock and add a chopped onion, a clove, a squeeze of lemon juice, 4 parsley stalks and ¼ teaspoon of salt. Simmer the stock for 30 minutes, then strain.

Clarified Butter

Clarified butter can be heated to a much higher temperature than ordinary butter. When butter is melted it separates into a clear yellow liquid and a milky residue which sinks. It is these milk particles which are responsible for ordinary butter burning at a much lower temperature. To prepare clarified butter, melt some butter in a pan, skim off the surface foam, and decant the crystal yellow liquid, the clarified butter. Discard the milky residue or stir it into soups or sauces.

Mayonnaise

If using olive oil to make mayonnaise, use a mild-tasting one such as Plagniol.

3 egg yolks	squeeze of lemon juice
1 level teaspoon mustard	14 fl oz/400 ml arachide
salt	(groundnut) oil

Whisk the egg yolks with the mustard, salt and lemon juice in a bowl with a balloon whisk. Whisk in the oil in a thin stream until the egg yolks are saturated and the mayonnaise is too thick. Thin it to the desired consistency with cold water. Too much water will diminish the richness of the sauce.

Bouquet Garni

A *bouquet garni* can either be tied together or enclosed in a small piece of muslin. Used to aromatize a dish, it consists of a few sprigs of parsley, a sprig of thyme and a bay leaf. Rosemary can be added for Provençal dishes.

Fines Herbes

A mixture of chopped parsley, chervil, tarragon and chives. Sadly, chervil is the least readily available of everyday-use herbs, and it is worth growing it if you can.

Chopping Herbs

Chopped herbs rapidly lose their flavour, and they should be chopped on the day they are required. Frozen herbs are a disaster; thyme, rosemary, tarragon and bay are fine dried. To finely chop leafy herbs, remove the leaves from the stalk and wash them. Using a large chopping board and a large knife, perform several rapid strokes of the knife to break the herbs down. Then, starting at one end of the pile and working gradually to the other end, chop them finely. Repeat this three times. Place the herbs in a clean tea-towel or piece of muslin and squeeze out any excess water.

Croûtons

Croûtons should be made freshly on the day they are to be used. Thinly slice some day-old French bread. Heat some olive oil or clarified butter in a frying-pan and cook the croûtons until they are golden-brown. Cool them on parchment paper before storing them.

If the croûtons are to accompany a particularly rich dish or be spread with a rich substance, lay them on a baking sheet and place it in the oven at 180°C/350°/Gas 4 for 5 minutes until they have dried out. Paint each side with olive oil or clarified butter, and return them to the oven for a further 10-12 minutes or until they are golden-brown. Cool them on parchment paper before storing them.

Tomatoes

Marmande tomatoes are ideal for skinning and deseeding. Cut a small cone from the top of the tomato, taking out the core. Slash a small cross on the base of each fruit and plunge them into boiling water for 30 seconds. Dunk them immediately into cold water. After a couple of minutes peel and deseed them.

Tomatoes can also be skinned without blanching them: quarter and deseed the tomato; with the skin face down on the chopping board, run a sharp, thin-bladed knife between the flesh and the skin. This method is undoubtedly quicker when preparing a small quantity of tomatoes; it also has an advantage over blanching in that there is no risk of cooking the surface flesh of the fruit.

Peppers

To grill peppers, see Salad of Roasted Peppers with Capers, p.108.

Squid

To prepare squid, see Risotto Nero, p. 54.

Mussels and Clams

To prepare mussels and clams, see Risotto Nero, p. 54.

Artichoke Hearts

To turn an artichoke, see Scallop and Artichoke Tartlets with Purée of Roasted Garlic, p. 32.

UTENSILS

Knives

A good set of chef's knives is essential for preparing food. You need a set, ranging in size from a heavy-bladed chopping knife with a 10-12/25-30 cm in blade, to a small paring knife. A filleting knife, a long thin-bladed smoked salmon knife and a serrated-edged bread knife will all be useful. A good set of knives lasts a lifetime and a feel for their use becomes second-nature, so that being without them in a kitchen can be quite disconcerting. Stainless steel blades are preferable to carbon steel; while carbon steel can be sharpened to a finer blade it wears down more quickly and oxidizes, blackening the blade. It must be greased when not in use to prevent it rusting. Sabatier knives are the most common chef's knives on sale in this country. There are a number of companies licensed to produce Sabatier knives, but only about four of these produce good quality knives. The Sabatier 'Jeune' knives which carry the grape emblem are perhaps the most commonly available and are good quality. German knives have the best reputation; Dreizack, Dick and Victorinox knives are to be recommended, in that order of preference. Dreizack are not that widely available, but can be obtained from David Mellor in Sloane Square who also have a catalogue and mail-order service. There is an element of personal taste here and one would do well to spend some time handling different knives to assess their feel before launching into a major purchase of any one range.

Chopping Boards

Keep several hard wooden chopping boards: two small boards (one for fruit, one for garlic and shallots), and a large one, about 22 × 14 in/60 × 35 cm, to be used for all other food preparation.

Saucepans

Saucepans come next on the list in importance after knives. A good set of heavy-bottomed stainless steel saucepans lasts a lifetime. I recommend Bourgeat pans, available from professional stockists. The base of the pans is heavier and more hard-wearing than its domestic counterparts, and heat is more evenly distributed.

Scales

For accuracy I recommend electronic scales, which convert to metric or imperial and register to the nearest ⅛ oz or gram.

Mandolin

A mandolin consists of two adjustable blades held in a wooden or steel frame. A folding support holds the mandolin at a tilt while slicing. The wooden models are not as effective. The stainless steel ones are relatively expensive, but durable, and quite apart from their practical use for thinly slicing vegetables or controlling the thickness of a slice, they are a beautifully designed instrument.

Mouli-Légumes

Used to purée food, this is a useful addition in the kitchen. For small quantities, however, the hassle of dismantling the apparatus, washing it and reassembling it far outweighs its usefulness, and in this case I recommend reducing the food to a coarse purée in a food processor and then pressing it through a sieve assisted by a 'sieve-pusher'; some of these resemble a hand-held garden-roller, or wooden mushroom, similar to the gadget your grandmother might have darned socks with.

Cake Tins

The most useful cake tins are the 'springform' variety, with a removable collar which clips on to the base. Keep a range of these in sizes varying from 7-10 in/18-25 cm. A loaf tin is essential, and you should also have a range of tart tins with removable bases.

Griddle Plate

My griddle plate is in constant use. It is a basic ridged iron grid which fits over a single gas ring on the stove. A word of caution, though: in the past I have cracked one of these using it on an electric plate. The griddle, like your best iron frying-pan, should be kept clean with a minimum of detergent or scouring — as a last resort take a wire brush to it. It must be properly dried to prevent it rusting. During the process of cooking, food may stick to the griddle and burn. In this case allow it to cool and clean it before continuing. It is essential to use one of these in conjunction with a powerful extractor fan or next to an open window. It would be folly to attempt to use one in a poorly ventilated kitchen.

Microwave

The history of the microwave is rewritten almost by the day, with new scares and scandals emerging constantly. I acquired one in order to heat small amounts of food for my baby, and it now has a definite, if limited, function in the kitchen, where it is used for melting butter and chocolate or heating something. I never use it for cooking and will gladly debate the disadvantages of cooking food in this fashion. Cooking involves a series of chemical reactions taking place, and the time something is cooked for is an important element. Cooking a dish in a microwave does not allow the flavours to develop and mingle as they would if it was conventionally cooked.

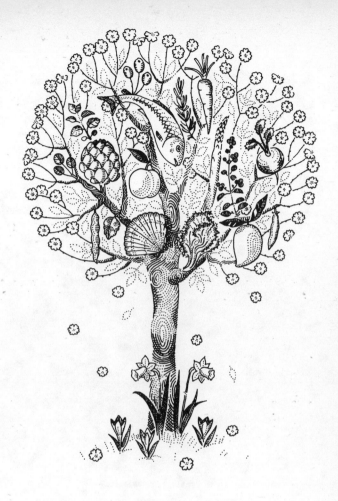

Spring

Menu 1: A Cold Buffet

Persian Omelette Served with Sour Cream

Sweet and Sour Aubergine

Purée of Butter Beans with Wilted Spinach

Green Salad

Farinata with Roasted Spices

Goat's Cheese Tart

Persian Omelette Served with Sour Cream

This recipe is adapted from Kukuye Sabsi, in *A New Book of Middle Eastern Food* by Claudia Roden. The *kuku* is a Persian omelette similar to an *eggah*, and is normally baked in the oven. It is traditionally served on New Year's Day in Iran, where its greenness is believed to be 'a symbol of fruitfulness in the coming year, bringing prosperity and happiness'. It is good served either hot or cold, with sour cream or Greek yoghurt, though the flavour of the herbs comes across best when it is served cold.

2 leeks	3 tablespoons chopped chervil,
4 spring onions	coriander and chives
4 oz/115 g watercress leaves	2 tablespoons walnuts
7 eggs	2 tablespoons sultanas
¾ oz/20 g butter	salt and pepper
2 tablespoons chopped parsley	5 fl oz/150 ml sour cream

Wash and dry the vegetables, trim them and chop them finely. Beat the eggs in a large bowl. Melt ½ oz/15 g of the butter in a frying-pan, add the leeks and onions and sweat them for a few minutes until they are soft, but not coloured. Stir them into the eggs. Melt the remaining butter and cook the watercress until it wilts; add this to the omelette mixture along with the chopped herbs. Coarsely chop the walnuts and sultanas and add them to the bowl; season generously with salt and pepper.

Butter a gratin dish and pour in the mixture to a depth of 1-1½ in/2.5-4 cm. Bake the omelette for 15-20 minutes at 200°C/400°F/ Gas 6. It should be golden and have risen when it is removed from the oven; if you like your omelette *baveuse*, keep an eye on it and remove it in time.

Serve it in wedges, with sour cream.

Sweet and Sour Aubergine

---

2 medium-sized aubergines	3 tablespoons aged red wine
salt and pepper	vinegar
olive oil for frying	1 tablespoon sugar
1 large red onion	1 tablespoon capers, chopped
6 tomatoes, skinned, seeded and	mint
chopped (or a 14 oz/400 g can	
tomatoes, drained)	

Slice the aubergines ¼ in/0.75 cm thick. Salt them liberally on each side and leave them to disgorge their bitter juices in a colander for 30 minutes; this reduces their absorbency when you come to fry them. Rinse the slices and pat them dry with kitchen paper.

Heat a few tablespoons of olive oil in a frying-pan, and fry the aubergine slices, a single layer at a time, till they are a deep brown. Arrange them on a plate.

Coarsely chop the onion. Heat a little olive oil in a saucepan, add the onion, and cook until it starts to turn golden. Add the tomatoes, vinegar, sugar, salt and pepper, taking into account that the aubergines are already seasoned with salt. Cook the sauce over a low heat until it is smooth and some of the liquid evaporates. Stir in the capers.

Spoon the sauce over the aubergine, and sprinkle it with chopped mint shortly before serving.

Purée of Butter Beans with Wilted Spinach

The spinach leaves should be young and tender. Skinned, dried broad beans can be used instead of butter beans, to give a coarser, marginally stronger, purée. They can be found in Italian or Spanish delicatessens. Butter beans produce a smoother, creamy purée which I prefer.

---

11 oz/310 g butter beans	salt and pepper
2 sticks celery, cut into lengths	12 oz/340 g spinach
1 small clove garlic	olive oil
6 tablespoons olive oil	

Soak the butter beans in plenty of water overnight. Drain and rinse them, and boil them with the celery for 1 hour, skimming the surface as necessary. Strain the beans and celery and purée them in an electric blender together with the garlic, olive oil, salt and pepper. You may find it easier to reduce them to a coarse purée in a food processor and then pass the purée through a sieve, or purée them through a mouli-légumes. The purée benefits from a generous addition of salt. Cover it with cling-film to prevent a hard surface forming as it cools.

Wash the spinach leaves well and dry them between two towels. Heat a little olive oil in a frying-pan, throw in some leaves, and toss them around until they just wilt. Remove them to a bowl and season them. Cook the rest of the spinach the same way, in batches.

When the bean purée and spinach are both tepid, mound the purée on a plate and arrange the spinach around it. Dribble over more olive oil before serving. An olive spoon, a small wooden ladle with a number of holes drilled in it, to be found in some kitchen-ware stores, is useful here. Alternatively you could use a long-spouted chrome olive-oil can, as typically found on the continent, which is useful wherever you need to control the flow of oil.

Green Salad

The green salad is an item that has particularly benefited from the emergence of new varieties of vegetables during recent years. Gone are the days of a bowl of limp lettuce, cress and thickly sliced cucumber by way of a green salad – at least, gone is the excuse for producing one.

Oak-leaf lettuce, lollo rosso, lollo biondo, cos, frisée, green batavia, escarole and mâche are just a few of the burgeoning brigade of lettuces now being sold. Sorrel, watercress, rocquette, radicchio, endive, baby spinach or dandelion may be on offer too; and herbs like chervil, lovage, red orach, parsley, chives or feathery fennel can be introduced to complement the accompanying dishes.

A green salad, or salad of mixed leaves, should consist of a happy combination of several different salad leaves, and herbs if desired, in such proportions that there is no one overwhelming flavour. The texture, flavour and appearance of the leaves should balance.

PREPARATION OF SALAD GREENS

When selecting a lettuce, be sure it is firm and crisp, at least in the centre. Ideally the salad should be prepared in the morning or the afternoon of the day it is to be used – it can be stored in a polythene bag in the fridge in its prepared state, but the stalk will begin to brown after a day. If you are intending to keep lettuce in this way, be sure to dry it thoroughly, as excess water will exacerbate the browning. Do not store it in the coldest section of the refrigerator.

Discard the outer leaves and any damaged ones. Discard too any coarse parts of the leaves inside with a leathery appearance, and any tough stalks. Cut or break up the remaining leaves. Some types of lettuce yield more than others in this process: you may salvage only a third of a cos lettuce, whereas an escarole can yield 95 per cent of perfect leaves. This is to be kept in mind if you wish to grow a selection of lettuces in a restricted space.

Wash the leaves in a sink full of cold water. Cleaning lettuce such as lollo rosso, which traps copious amounts of soil and bugs in the folds of its leaves, can be aided by the addition of a shot of vinegar to the water. Dry the lettuce well and store it in a polythene bag in the fridge until it is required.

When you come to serve the salad, it should be tossed by hand in a bowl so that each leaf is lightly coated with dressing. There should not be a pool of dressing in the bottom of the bowl. Remove the leaves to the bowl or plate from which it is to be served. A salad with a predominance of lamb's lettuce will benefit if dressed with the oil first, the vinegar then being splashed over.

Vinaigrette

My preferred vinaigrette for a plain green salad is well flavoured with garlic, made with a flavourful extra virgin olive oil, and with the possible addition of a 'chapon' beneath the salad – a croûton rubbed with garlic and sprinkled with olive oil (see Olive Oil, p. 9).

The ratio of vinegar to oil should be at least 1:8, on occasions 1:10, particularly if you are using balsamic vinegar. Sherry vinegar, red wine vinegar, white wine vinegar, raspberry, tarragon and balsamic vinegar are all possibilities, or if it is a particularly good olive oil then just a squeeze of lemon juice will do. An unexciting wine vinegar can be jazzed up with the addition of sprigs of herbs, peppercorns or lemon zest, and left for a few days.

Hazelnut and walnut oils, which should be stored in the fridge, are useful too. Hazelnut is the nuttier of the two; I prefer walnut oil, as hazelnut oil can be quite cloying. Both oils should be used in conjunction with a flavourless oil; they can be too strong and pervasive otherwise.

Olive Oil Vinaigrette with Garlic

½ small clove garlic	1 tablespoon sherry vinegar
⅓ teaspoon salt	8 tablespoons extra virgin olive oil

Using the flat edge of a knife, crush the garlic together with the salt so that it forms a paste. Whisk this with the vinegar until well combined. Whisk in the olive oil.

Nut Oil Vinaigrette

⅓ teaspoon salt	4 tablespoons arachide
¼ teaspoon mustard	(groundnut) oil or other
1 tablespoon sherry vinegar	tasteless oil
4 tablespoons hazelnut or walnut oil	

Whisk together the salt, mustard and vinegar until the salt dissolves. Whisk in the oils.

Farinata with Roasted Spices

Farinata has a wonderfully eccentric flavour. It is a type of round, thick pancake made with chickpea flour. It is a speciality of Liguria in Italy and is normally consumed in bars or on the street rather than in homes. The first time I made farinata I used a Swiss roll tin, for want of better equipment, and the result was a thin pancake, about ⅛ in/0.5 cm thick, instead of the ½ in/1.25 cm it should have been. After experimenting with both thick and thin farinatas, I concluded that a thin one would be right as part of a *mezze* or *antipasto* and is more appropriate to this menu, and the thicker one should accompany braised vegetables or a soup. A thick farinata will require a longer cooking time than the thin one, closer to 40 minutes.

Chickpea flour is available in Spanish or Italian delicatessens, healthfood shops and Indian shops, where it is called gram flour or *besan*. This is a useful recipe for someone who cannot eat wheat flour or yeast.

8 oz/225 g chickpea flour	*6 tablespoons olive oil*
1 level teaspoon salt	*ground black pepper*
14 fl oz/400 ml cold water	

Mix together the chickpea flour, salt and water, adding the water a little at a time to avoid lumps. Rest the resulting thin batter for several hours or even overnight so that the flour is completely slaked. This period of soaking is important.

Preheat the oven to 220°C/425°F/Gas 7. Skim the surface foam from the batter and any other liquid floating on the surface beneath it. Take a Swiss roll tin (13 × 9 in/33 × 23 cm) and measure the olive oil into it. Pour in the batter and amalgamate the two as thoroughly as possible. Place the farinata into the hot oven for 30 minutes, until the top is golden. It will hiss as it cooks. The sides of the farinata will shrink from the sides of the tin and the surface will be oily. Grind a fair amount of black pepper over it and serve it cut into wedges while it is still warm.

Dukkah (roasted spices)

Despite its Italian origins, farinata strikes me as peculiarly Middle Eastern in quality, although I have not come across a Middle Eastern equivalent. It is perfect paired with a bowl of olive oil and some dukkah, to dunk it in one and then the other. Dukkah is an Egyptian speciality, a mixture of roasted nuts and spices, coarsely crushed. The recipe is often a family tradition and each will have its own interpretation.

1½ oz/45 g sesame seeds	*¾ oz/20 g hazelnuts*
1 oz/30 g coriander seeds	*½ oz/15 g cumin seeds*
	salt and pepper

Preheat the oven to 200°C/400°F/Gas 6. Roast the ingredients separately for around 7 minutes, and pound them together in a pestle and mortar, adding the seasoning, until you have a coarse mixture. An electric coffee grinder could be used, though mine is too efficient and even a single burst renders the mixture too powdery. The dukkah can be stored in an airtight container for several weeks.

Goat's Cheese Tart

Base

2 oz/55 g chilled butter	*¾ oz/20 g plain flour*
3 oz/85 g ground almonds	*½ oz/15 g icing sugar*

Filling

1 oz/30 g vanilla sugar	*1 egg, separated*
1½ oz/ 45 g caster sugar	*5 fl oz/150 ml double cream*
12 oz/340 g fresh unsalted goat's cheese	*1 tablespoon flaked almonds*
	icing sugar
1 egg yolk	

Process the ingredients for the base of the cheesecake into a ball in a food processor. Press the dough into an 8-in/20-cm springform cake tin, making the sides 1½ in/4 cm deep; sprinkle the dough with a little flour as you work if it is sticky. Chill for 30 minutes, then bake the base for 12-15 minutes at 170°C/325°F/Gas 3.

Beat the sugars and goat's cheese together. Add the egg yolks and the cream. Stiffly whisk the egg white and incorporate it into the cheese mixture. Pour this into the base and scatter the surface with the flaked almonds. Bake the cheesecake for 35 minutes at 170°C/325°F/Gas 3, until it is turning golden.

When it is cool, remove the springform collar and trim the pastry to the same level as the filling. Chill the tart and sprinkle it with icing sugar before serving.

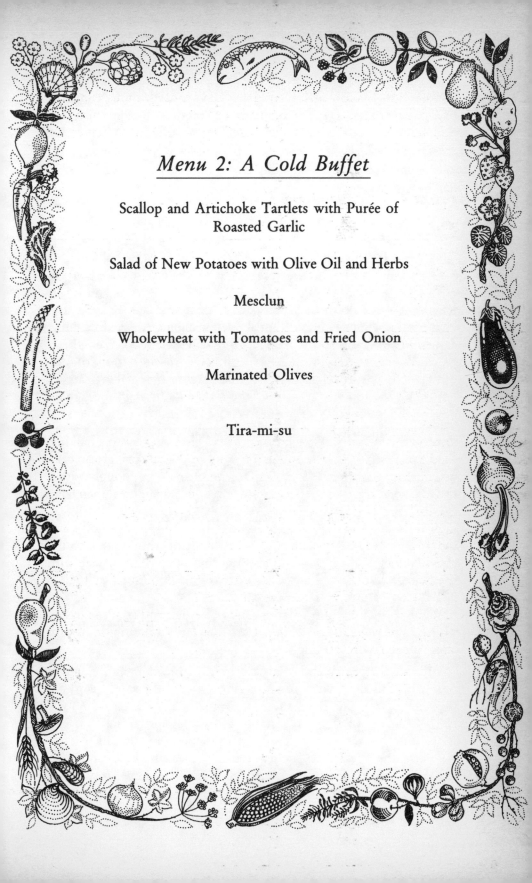

Menu 2: A Cold Buffet

Scallop and Artichoke Tartlets with Purée of
Roasted Garlic

Salad of New Potatoes with Olive Oil and Herbs

Mesclun

Wholewheat with Tomatoes and Fried Onion

Marinated Olives

Tira-mi-su

Scallop and Artichoke Tartlets with Purée of Roasted Garlic

See p. 197 for scallops. Jerusalem artichokes can be used instead of globe artichokes — it loses a couple of points on presentation but is just as good to eat.

TO TURN AN ARTICHOKE

Equip yourself with a small paring knife and a bowl of lemon juice or vinegar. Place a kitchen bin close by. Cut off the stalk of the artichoke and, starting at the base, cut away the coarse outer leaves, dipping the exposed flesh in the lemon juice or vinegar as you work to prevent it discolouring. When you have cut around the sides, slice off the top to about ½ in/1.25 cm above the choke. Alternatively the choke can be cut out at this stage; scrape away the pitted layer where the choke was rooted to the heart using a teaspoon — it discolours rapidly on exposure to air. Tidy the sides and the base, taking care to remove all the tough stalk. Leave the artichoke heart in the lemon juice or vinegar until you are ready to cook it.

To cook the artichoke, bring a large pan of water to the boil, acidulate it and cook the hearts for 15-20 minutes. Cool them in a basin of cold water. Pull out the inner artichoke leaves, and use a teaspoon to remove the fibrous choke if you have not already done so. It should come away quite easily. If it is stubborn and will not come loose, it may require a little further cooking.

9 oz/255 g puff pastry	12 large scallops
1 head of garlic	olive oil
1 large red pepper	¼ teaspoon chilli paste, or knife
4 globe artichokes	tip of finely chopped fresh
4 tablespoons single cream	chilli
salt and pepper	finely chopped parsley and basil
lemon juice	

Thinly roll the pastry and line six 4-in/10-cm tartlet cases. Weight these with foil and baking beans, securing the tartlet sides firmly to the sides of the tin. Bake the cases for 20-25 minutes at 160°C/325°F/Gas 3 until they are totally cooked. Remove the foil and beans and cool the cases; then remove them from the tins.

Preheat the oven to its highest setting. Roast the head of garlic, whole, and the pepper for 20 minutes. Place the pepper inside two polythene bags, one inside the other, secure the opening and allow it to cool. Skin and deseed the pepper and cut it into thin strips. When the garlic is cool enough to handle, squeeze each clove from its casing into a pestle and mortar.

Turn and cook the artichokes as described above, leaving the leaves intact. Remove the artichoke leaves, scraping the flesh from the best endowed of them into the pestle and mortar with the garlic. Remove the chokes, and trim each heart. Slice them thinly.

Pound the garlic and artichoke flesh together, adding the cream gradually. Season the purée with salt, pepper and lemon juice to taste.

Remove the gristle at the side of each scallop. Avoid washing the scallops and try to scrape them with a knife instead. Halve each one, brush on all sides with olive oil and season them. Heat a cast-iron frying-pan until it is smoking hot, lay the scallops on the base of the pan. The exterior should seal and caramelize almost instantly; turn them, using a palette knife, and cook them momentarily until this side caramelizes also. Squeeze a little lemon juice over them.

In a bowl toss the sliced artichokes, red pepper and scallops together with a little olive oil, the chilli paste and some salt. Sprinkle a little chopped parsley into this and just a suggestion of chopped basil.

Spread the base of each tartlet with the garlic purée, and arrange some of the scallop and artichoke in the centre of each one. You could tuck a couple of small leaves of basil into each tartlet if you wish.

Salad of New Potatoes with Olive Oil and Herbs

Obtaining herbs remains a problem. It is normally possible to find a selection of three or four, but not necessarily the same three or four you set out to buy. The combination below is intended as guidance rather than a decree.

1½ lb/0.7 kg new potatoes	4 tablespoons chopped herbs
2 tablespoons white wine	(basil, coriander, parsley,
9 tablespoons olive oil	chervil, chives)
	salt and pepper

Scrub the potatoes and boil them for 10-15 minutes until they are just cooked. Slice them warm into a bowl. Pour over the wine and olive oil. Mix in the herbs and seasoning.

The salad is at its best after 24 hours, when the flavours have had a chance to develop.

Mesclun

Mesclun originated in Southern France, where the Niçoise word *mesclumo* means a mixture. It consists of a mixture of leaves, including those of wild plants. Dandelion, chervil, rocquette, chicory, lamb's lettuce, salsify, groundsel, purslane, and oak-leaf lettuce are all typical leaves in mesclun. Its slightly bitter taste marries well with other indigenous Provençal ingredients: goat's cheese, sun-dried tomatoes, garlic, pine-nuts, olives and anchovies. It is also native to Rome and the Rouergue, and in the past I have found it being sold in large boxes in the vast indoor food market in Florence, while searching for victuals for a Tuscan picnic later in the day.

All too often mesclun turns up in a less than authentic form in London restaurants, consisting of a rather boring combination of mixed salad leaves. When I talked to one of the largest herb and vegetable suppliers to the restaurant trade in London I began to understand why, as they reeled off a handful of tame varieties of lettuce they used to make up mesclun. This aside, mesclun does seem to be rather an abused item on the menu: 'Let them eat mesclun, and let them pay for it.'

Wholewheat with Tomatoes and Fried Onion

6 oz/170 g wholewheat
4 tablespoons garlic vinaigrette
   (see p. 28)
2 onions

oil for deep-frying
¾ lb/340 g tomatoes
salt, pepper and sugar

Boil the wholewheat in water for 50 minutes. Toss it with the vinaigrette while it is still hot.

Halve each onion and shave it finely into crescents (a mandolin would be helpful here). Heat plenty of oil in a pan and deep-fry the onion to dark golden strands. When they are cool and crisp toss half of them into the wholewheat. Mound this in the centre of a dish.

Blanch and peel the tomatoes (see p. 16), then slice them thinly and arrange them around the outside of the dish. Season the tomatoes with salt, pepper and a pinch of sugar. Scatter the remaining onion over the salad.

The salad can also be served omitting the onions, with a few shavings of Parmesan or provolone cheese scattered over it.

Marinated Olives

Marinating is a good ruse for invigorating otherwise boring olives; though no amount of artistry will make a bad olive good.

1 lb/450 g olives	*1 sprig fennel (or ¼ teaspoon*
½ pint/300 ml olive oil	*fennel seeds)*
1 small onion, cut into 8 sections	*2 sprigs thyme*
3-4 cloves garlic, halved	*2-in/5-cm strip orange peel*
2 bay leaves	*½ teaspoon coriander seeds*

Combine all the ingredients together in a jar and leave them to marinate for 48 hours or longer.

Tira-mi-su

Despite its recent origin, Tira-mi-su rose to cult status with alacrity. I would wager it is here to stay and not just a passing fancy; it is a seriously delicious dessert.

Literally it means 'pick me up', and it must contain coffee and liqueur to qualify for this. This recipe uses Kahlua, a Mexican coffee liqueur, but brandy, rum, Cointreau, Tia Maria, a combination of some of these, or others, could be used.

Should the occasion lend itself, make this in treble quantity or more, in your largest, most beautiful bowl. Together with a tart, a fruit and a chocolate dish you have a good dessert selection for a large number of guests.

6 fl oz/175 ml strong fresh black coffee	*1 oz/30 g caster sugar*
	1 oz/30 g vanilla sugar
3 fl oz/85 ml Kahlua or other liqueur	*1 lb/450 g mascarpone*
	1 packet sponge fingers or savoiardi
3 eggs	*cocoa for dusting*

Make the coffee and allow it to cool. Combine it with the liqueur in a shallow bowl.

Separate the eggs. Whisk the sugars and the egg yolks together. Beat in the mascarpone, beating it well until no lumps remain. Whisk the egg whites and fold them deftly into the mascarpone mixture.

Smear a spoon or two of the mascarpone mousse around the bowl, or bowls, in which it is to be served. Dip the sponge fingers one at a time into the coffee-liqueur mixture until the sponge just starts to yield between your fingers, but not so that it is totally sodden.

Cover the base of the bowl with a single layer of sponge fingers. Smooth some mascarpone mousse on top of this. There will be three layers of sponge and of mousse, and as you layer the two you should take into account that if the bowl has sloping sides, nearly half the mousse may be required for the top layer. Smooth the top with a palette knife.

Chill the Tira-mi-su for at least 2 hours, preferably overnight. Dust the surface with cocoa shortly before serving.

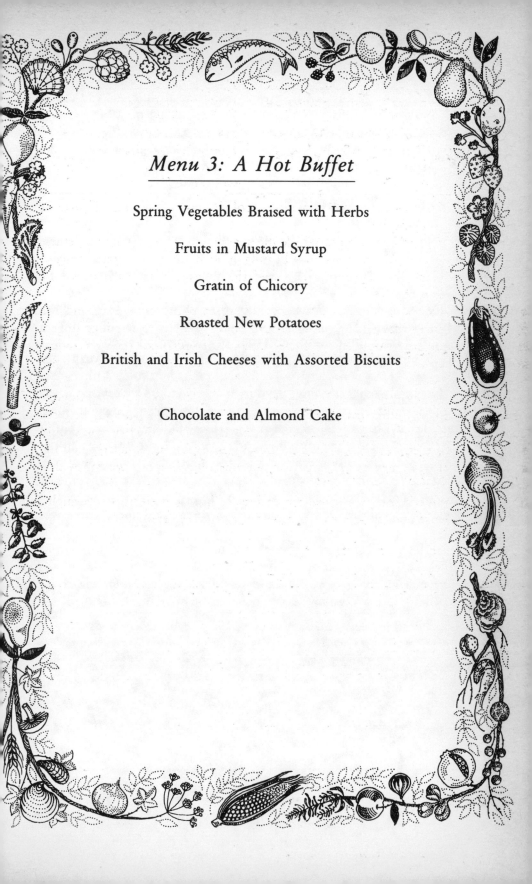

Menu 3: A Hot Buffet

Spring Vegetables Braised with Herbs

Fruits in Mustard Syrup

Gratin of Chicory

Roasted New Potatoes

British and Irish Cheeses with Assorted Biscuits

Chocolate and Almond Cake

This menu is more suitable for supper than for dinner, and can be produced in quantity with relative ease, laid out on a big table for people to help themselves. However, it is also more suited to 'laps' than to standing up, fork in one hand, glass in the other, so this ought to be taken into consideration.

Spring Vegetables Braised with Herbs

There is an element of gimmick or fad attached to 'baby' vegetables. Perfected by the French, the baby vegetables grown in France are a different variety of vegetable from the larger specimens, and are fully grown in miniature. Efforts to grow them in this country have proved only partially successful. On the whole, English baby vegetables are simply the large varieties harvested young, and they do not have the colour or flavour of the special varieties.

Some baby vegetables are sweeter and more tender than their normal-sized counterparts, with accentuated flavour. Others lack the texture, character and flavour. It is wise to be aware that size is not necessarily an indication of flavour. Suppliers to the restaurant trade can offer a wide choice of vegetables in miniature: baby purple aubergines, baby yellow aubergines, baby red beetroot, baby golden beetroot, and baby carrots, cabbages, cauliflower, corn, courgettes, cucumbers, artichokes, fennel, leeks and turnips are just some on offer. You are unlikely to find this wide variety of infant vegetables in your local supermarket, but more and more are finding their way on to the shelves.

The purpose of this casserole is to use whatever young spring vegetables are at hand; if this includes some sweet and tender baby vegetables then so much the better. The vegetables in the recipe below were a random selection from the supermarket.

½ oz/15g dried wild mushrooms	3 oz/85 g broad beans, podded
6 baby turnips, with tops	and skinned (use frozen if
6 baby carrots, with tops	fresh are unavailable)
3 bulbs baby fennel	12 baby corn
2 oz/55 g green beans	6 sprigs of tarragon
1 heart of celery	6 sprigs of thyme
1 small cauliflower	12 small cloves garlic, peeled, or 6
8 spring onions	large cloves, halved
4 oz/115 g asparagus	salt and pepper
3 oz/85 g sugar snap peas	8 tablespoons olive oil
	8 tablespoons white wine

Cover the dried mushrooms with boiling water and soak them for 15 minutes.

Place each vegetable as it is cooked into a casserole or deep roasting tray. Trim the tops of the turnips and carrots; peel the turnips and boil them in salted water for 2-3 minutes, boil the carrots for 4 minutes. Trim the fennel bulbs, halve them vertically and boil them for 3-4 minutes.

Trim the green beans, cut the celery into 2-in/5-cm lengths, discarding the leaves, and break the cauliflower into florets; boil each vegetable for 2 minutes. Trim the roots of the spring onions and leave 1 in/2.5 cm of green shoots; boil them for 1 minute. Trim the asparagus and sugar snaps and cook them for 1 minute each. If the broad beans are fresh, boil them for 1 minute. Add the baby corn to the casserole.

Drain the soaked mushrooms, straining the liquid through a fine-mesh sieve or muslin, and reserving it. Add the herbs, garlic and mushrooms to the casserole. Season well with salt and pepper. Pour over the liquid in which the mushrooms soaked, the olive oil and the white wine. The recipe can be prepared in advance to this point.

Cover the casserole and bake it at 170°C/325°F/Gas 3 for about 25-35 minutes. Stir the casserole after 15 minutes. Remove it from the oven 5 minutes before the meal is to be served. Drain the liquid from the vegetables into a small saucepan and reduce it by half, then pour it back over the vegetables.

Fruits in Mustard Syrup

Fruits in mustard-flavoured syrup, or *mostarda di frutta*, is a regional speciality from Cremona in northern Italy. It is a relish made with candied fruits cooked in a white wine and honey syrup containing essence of mustard — *senape*. A bowl of this relish looks particularly attractive, an assortment of translucent, amber-coloured fruits in a thick, clear syrup. The *mostarda di frutta* I have found in Italian and Spanish delicatessens over here contains apricots, cherries and pears; but peaches, apples, pumpkin, melon, figs, plums and small oranges are also suitable.

If you are unable to obtain this relish, substitute another chutney or relish. Essentially the domain of the domestic kitchen, try and lay your hands on a jar of home-made something.

Gratin of Chicory

6 heads of chicory	8 fl oz/225 ml double cream
salt and pepper	

Halve the chicory heads vertically and remove the core. Cut each half into thin vertical strips and place them in a gratin dish. Season the cream and pour it over the chicory. Cook the gratin for 1 hour at 170°C/325°F/Gas 3; stir it after 30 minutes.

Roasted New Potatoes

This is one of the simplest ways of cooking potatoes, and one of the most versatile. A rich and flavourful jacket gives way to a melting interior. The herbs can be omitted if they do not fit in with the scheme of things, or another herb or some garlic can be used instead. They are delicious as substantial cocktail party food, accompanied by a bowl of aioli, Romesco or skordalia.

1½ lb/65 g new potatoes	1 heaped dessertspoon fresh
olive oil	thyme
	coarse grain sea salt

Scrub the potatoes and parboil them for 10 minutes. Place them in a roasting tray. Dribble over some olive oil, and scatter over the thyme and some sea salt. Roast the potatoes for 1 hour at 170°C/325°F/Gas 3.

British and Irish Cheeses with Assorted Biscuits

A trip to the local delicatessen to buy cheeses during the 1970s would have you pondering over labels like Brie, Camembert, Port-Salut, Roquefort and Gruyère, basically a selection of established French cheeses with a few English and Swiss thrown in. Today you can also expect to be confronted by an exciting group of virtual strangers: Desmond and Gabriel, Lavistown, Cooleeney, Mileens, Mendip, Perrouche, Spenwood, Devon Garland and Cashel Blue, all of which are British cheeses. The 1970s witnessed the first wave in a resurgence of the small cheesemaker. There were those farming small herds of between twenty and thirty cattle for whom it was not profitable simply to sell the milk, and those who just wanted to start making cheese and dedicated themselves to it. Simultaneously many traditional producers, under pressure to effect economies of scale and produce ever cheaper cheese, were either closing down or scaling up. These new producers managed to establish a market, and the mid-1980s saw a second wave of new producers, who could now see the market and were tempted by the premium attached to this type of product, which they could not achieve by selling the milk. Some of those motivated purely by money failed to come up with the goods, but enough good new cheeses emerged to present an impressive range collectively.

Now the market is established, one of the growing problems is quotas. For many small cheese producers, the demand for their cheeses now outstrips the quantity they are by law able to produce, particularly since America has opened up as a market. Hopefully they will be regrouped outside the current system to allow them to develop to their full potential.

Cheese remains a 'grey' area for the vegetarian. About a quarter of farm-produced English cheeses currently use vegetarian rennet. Considerable development has been carried out recently to improve it; in the past it has affected the quality of the cheese, particularly mature cheeses. The sinister specimens which lurk in the fridges of healthfood shops have firmly prejudiced my opinion of vegetarian rennet. It is encouraging to know that these may soon disappear, or at least improve, and increase the number of farm-produced vegetarian cheeses.

There is strong statistical evidence to suggest that unpasteurized cheeses were used as a Government scapegoat for cases of listeria food poisoning in 1989. Recorded cases of food poisoning from cheese during recent decades represent a fractional percentage of the total number of cases, and half the cases of listeria in cheese can be traced to pasteurized milk. Experiments currently under way in this field indicate that unpasteurized milk has a natural immunity to the vast proliferation of bugs which pasteurized milk does not. Until recently nearly all the Cheshire and Lancashire cheese produced in this country was made with unpasteurized milk, although it was not an advertised fact.

The outstanding impression of farm-produced British cheeses is their quality. Collectively they are totally different in character from French or Spanish cheeses. 'Affineur' Randolph Hodgson, of Neal's Yard Dairy, sees French cheeses as being 'wild' and British ones as more restrained, controlled but still interesting, the stiff upper lip almost woven into the recipe.

The British Isles are bestowed with rich, varied pastures, and this is the foundation for good milk. Careful husbandry of the land, of the animals, and good milking methods also contribute to good milk. No cheesemaker, however good, will produce good cheese with lousy milk. Most small cheesemakers produce their own milk and look after their animals and land. There are very few truly organic cheeses which carry the Soil Association symbol, but many are nearly organic: the farmer may practise organic farming but buy in feed such as ordinary hay during the winter. There are many variables involved in this type of cheese production, and it can differ from day to day even with the most closely standardized conditions. The season, the area, the pasture, the breed of the cow, the milking methods and the starter will all add specific character to a cheese.

The ideal place to store cheese is under cellar-like conditions, somewhere not too stuffy, though not in a draught, and there should be a dampness in the air; humidity is almost more important than temperature. If a cheese is cracking it needs to be in moister conditions; a last resort is a damp tea-towel. Cut cheeses are better wrapped in waxed paper than cling-film, which suffocates them. A fridge is too dry and too cold. Cheeses will mature at different temperatures, and ideally a cheese should be eaten at its maturing temperature; to keep a cheese from over-ripening the temperature can be reduced, but it should be brought back to the maturing temperature before it is eaten. The good cheese months, like those of shellfish, are the months with an 'r'. Traditional hard cheeses with a natural rind mature to a stable product; moisture has evaporated and its acidity preserves it. Soft cheeses are volatile and need to be eaten quickly. Cheeses vary from batch to batch and conditions change constantly, so the basic rule is to check cheese frequently and react to what it needs.

Assorted Biscuits: Oatmeal Biscuits, Sesame Biscuits, Wheatmeal Crackers

Home-made biscuits to accompany cheese are not something many people have time to churn out as a matter of course. But for a special occasion, when you have gone to the trouble of shopping for a good selection of cheeses, it is well worth spending an evening during the preceding week or two to produce a batch. They are always appreciated.

The oatmeal and sesame biscuits are thin and delicate; the wheatmeal crackers are thicker and well suited to hard cheeses.

There are a number of brands of vegetarian 'suet' on the market, any of which can be used here. All these biscuits will keep well in an airtight container for several weeks.

Oatmeal Biscuits

(makes 2-3 dozen)

6 oz/170 g medium oatmeal	1 level teaspoon salt
4 oz/115 g plain flour	2 oz/55 g white cooking fat
¼ teaspoon bicarbonate of soda	boiling water
	oatmeal for rolling

Place the dry ingredients together in the bowl of a food processor and incorporate the cooking fat. Bring the dough together with boiling water and knead it to distribute the fat evenly. Wrap it in cling-film and rest it in the fridge for an hour.

Preheat the oven to 140°C/275°F/Gas 1. Keep the dough moist to facilitate the rolling, and sprinkle it with oatmeal as you roll it. Roll it as thinly as possible. Cut it into 3-in/7.5-cm squares, and halve these to form triangles. Alternatively use a biscuit cutter.

Place the biscuits on a baking sheet and bake them for 30 minutes. This time will differ from oven to oven; the biscuits should be crisp but not coloured, and just starting to brown. Allow them to cool before storing them in an airtight container.

Sesame Biscuits

(makes 2-3 dozen)

6 oz/170 g sesame seeds	1 level teaspoon salt
4 oz/115 g plain flour	2 oz/55 g white cooking fat
¼ teaspoon bicarbonate of soda	boiling water
	sesame seeds for rolling

Place the sesame seeds in an electric coffee grinder, and give it a short burst to break up some of the seeds without reducing them to a powder. Repeat this with the seeds to be used for rolling the dough. Combine the 6 oz/170 g of sesame seeds with the other dry ingredients in the bowl of a food processor. Incorporate the fat. Bring the dough together with boiling water. Wrap it in cling-film and rest it in the fridge for an hour.

Preheat the oven to 140°C/275°F/Gas 1. Dust the worktop with some of the remaining sesame seeds and roll the dough as thinly as possible, scattering it with more crushed seeds as required. Cut the dough into squares or triangles with a sharp knife. Lift the biscuits on to baking sheets using a palette knife.

Bake the biscuits, following the instructions for cooking oatmeal biscuits above.

Wheatmeal Crackers

(makes 3-4 dozen)

6 oz/170 g wholemeal flour	½ teaspoon sugar
4 oz/115 g plain flour	4 oz/115 g butter
2 level teaspoons baking powder	¼ teaspoon wholegrain mustard
½ teaspoon bicarbonate of soda	4 tablespoons natural yoghurt
½ teaspoon salt	

Place the dry ingredients together in the bowl of a food processor. Add the butter, cut into pieces, and process the ingredients. Add the mustard and yoghurt. Bring the dough together with a little cold water if necessary. Wrap it in cling-film and rest it in the fridge for an hour.

Preheat the oven to 180°C/350°F/Gas 4. Dust the worktop with wholemeal flour, and roll the dough ⅛ in/0.5 cm thick. Cut it into rounds using a 3-in/7.5-cm fluted biscuit cutter. Bake the 'scones' for 10-12 minutes, until they are risen and just starting to change colour.

Turn the oven down to 150°C/300°F/Gas 2. Split the scones in two horizontally, and place them on a baking sheet, cut side up. Return them to the oven for 25 minutes, until they are crisp and just starting to change colour.

Chocolate and Almond Cake

This cake has all the qualities of a 'gâteau' without the drawbacks. It is essentially quick and easy to make, it is pleasantly rich without being too sweet or sickly, and it looks very pretty without being wildly elaborate.

The recipe uses the same chocolate cream for the top and sides of the cake as between the layers. A good variation is to sandwich the layers with praline cream (see recipe below), to which you can add raspberries or wild strawberries. In that case, half the amount of chocolate cream would be required for the exterior of the cake.

Chocolate cream

8 oz/225 g bitter chocolate	3×5 fl oz/150 ml cartons sour cream

Cake

6 eggs, separated	12 oz/340 g ground almonds
9 oz/255 g caster sugar	1½ teaspoons baking powder

To decorate

chocolate leaves, curls or shavings

Preheat the oven to 180°C/350°F/Gas 4.

Melt the chocolate in a double boiler. Beat the sour cream into the chocolate. Chill for 2 hours.

Whisk together the egg yolks and sugar – the mixture should not be too pale and thick. Stiffly whisk the egg whites and fold them into the mixture. Add the ground almonds and the baking powder.

Butter two 9-in/23-cm springform cake tins. Pour two-thirds of the cake mixture into one tin, and the remaining third into the other.

Bake the larger cake for 40 minutes and the smaller for 25 minutes, until a skewer comes out clean from the centre of each one. Remove the collars from the cakes and cool them.

Cut the larger cake in half horizontally. Slice the brown surface off the smaller cake, and slice the cake off the bottom of the tin, leaving the brown base.

Layer the cake with the chocolate cream, using the smaller cake as the middle layer. Coat the top and sides of the cake with the cream, and decorate it with chocolate leaves, curls or shavings.

Praline Cream

Try to find chopped, toasted hazelnuts. Otherwise you could toast some skinned almonds. Hazelnuts can be skinned by first toasting them and then rubbing the skins off using a clean tea-towel, but this is rather laborious. One short cut is to buy nut brittle or praline from a sweet counter.

3 oz/85 g sugar	2 oz/55 g toasted, chopped
2 fl oz/55 ml water	hazelnuts
	1/2 pint/300 ml double cream

Make a caramel with the sugar and water by placing them together in a saucepan. Swirl the solution until the sugar dissolves. Cook it for 3-4 minutes until it turns the colour of ale, swirling it occasionally. Stir in the nuts and pour the mixture on to a buttered baking sheet. When it hardens, after about 10 minutes, cover it with a tea-towel and crush it using a rolling pin. (This task is beyond the intended use of a domestic food processor, and will not do the blade any good.) The concrete surface of the back yard or some paving stones are a good place for crushing praline. Here you can smash away without alarming anyone.

Stiffly whip the cream and fold in the praline.

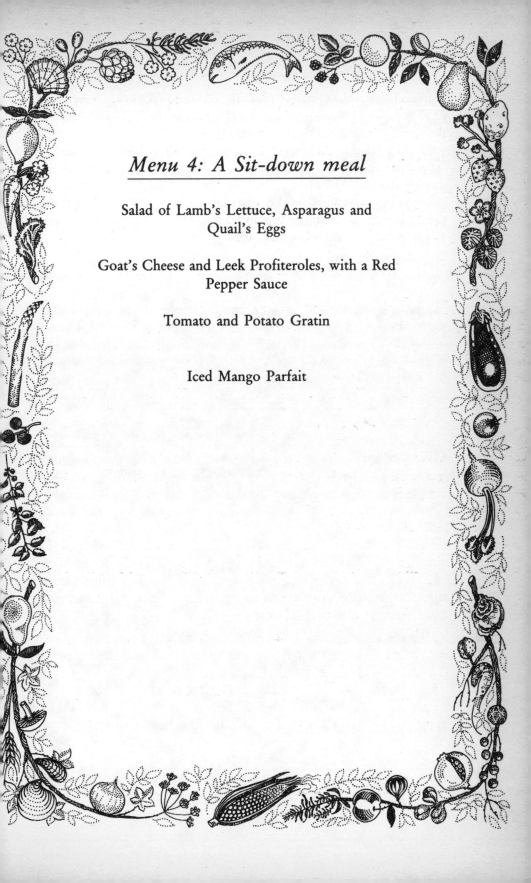

Menu 4: A Sit-down meal

Salad of Lamb's Lettuce, Asparagus and
Quail's Eggs

Goat's Cheese and Leek Profiteroles, with a Red
Pepper Sauce

Tomato and Potato Gratin

Iced Mango Parfait

Salad of Lamb's Lettuce, Asparagus and Quail's Eggs

The season for home-grown asparagus is so short, and it is so good, that it seems better to over-indulge for two months and forget it for the following ten. It is at its best when very fresh, and you should look for spears with a minimum of open scales, avoiding any yellowness of the stalk. Peel the stalk where the skin visibly becomes thicker. Keep the ends for soup. Too often asparagus is overcooked: it should not be crunchy, but should be slightly resistant to the bite. Some asparagus, particularly thin sprue, is cooked in as little as 3 minutes.

Lamb's lettuce is the most delicate of salad leaves. Its small, tongue-shaped leaves are a rich viridian green, tender with a velvety texture. They absorb oil quickly, and once dressed will not abide much standing around.

Vinaigrette

1 dessertspoon tarragon vinegar	4 dessertspoons arachide
1/4 teaspoon mustard	(groundnut) oil
1/3 teaspoon salt	4 dessertspoons olive oil
	1/2 teaspoon finely chopped
	tarragon

Salad

9 oz/250 g asparagus spears	6 oz/170 g lamb's lettuce
salt and pepper	18 quail's eggs

To make the vinaigrette, whisk together the vinegar, mustard and salt, until the salt dissolves. Whisk in the oils and add the tarragon.

Trim the asparagus, tie it into bundles and cook it in boiling salted water. Test it to see if it is cooked by inserting a knife half-way down a spear. Plunge the asparagus into cold water.

Remove the roots from the lamb's lettuce by twisting them from the leaves, and wash it thoroughly in a sink of cold water, taking care to remove all the grit. Dry it gently between two tea-towels.

Boil the quail's eggs for 2½ minutes, then plunge them into cold water. Cut one in half to check that they are sufficiently cooked. The yolk should be cooked on the outside and moist within. Care and dexterity are the best tools when shelling quail's eggs. A small sharp knife can help to break the membrane initially. I normally cook more quail's eggs than will be needed, to allow for disasters. Once peeled, they can be immersed in cold water in a bowl until required.

Toss the asparagus and lamb's lettuce with the vinaigrette in a bowl by hand. Arrange on individual plates. Halve the quail's eggs and arrange them over the salad. Alternatively compose the salad on a large platter. Equip the table with a peppermill and some salt.

Goat's Cheese and Leek Profiteroles, with a Red Pepper Sauce

Inspiration for this dish comes from *The Natural Cuisine of Georges Blanc*, a book of stunning recipes and photographs, centred on seasonal fruits and vegetables.

Sauce

3 small red peppers	1 dessertspoon balsamic vinegar
2 shallots	10 fl oz/275 ml double-strength
1 clove garlic	vegetable stock
2 tablespoons olive oil	1 oz/30 g butter
2 tablespoons tomato concassée	salt and pepper

Profiteroles

6½ fl oz/190 ml water	2½ oz/70 g flour
2 oz/55 g butter	3 eggs (size 5) and 1 beaten egg to
pinch each of sugar and salt	glaze

Filling

1 lb/450 g leeks	4 oz/115 g mature goat's cheese
1 oz/30 g butter	½ teaspoon Dijon mustard
2 fl oz/55 ml white wine	1½ oz/45 g pine nuts
3 fl oz/85 ml double cream	salt and pepper

Garnish

baby leeks (if the baby leeks are the size of spring onions allow 3 per person, if they are larger allow one leek per person and cut it into strips)

Peel the peppers using a potato peeler; core them and remove any seeds. Cut them roughly into dice.

Finely chop the shallots and garlic. Heat the olive oil in a saucepan and sweat the shallots and garlic for a couple of minutes; add the diced red pepper and cook for 8 minutes more. Add the tomato and the balsamic vinegar and continue to cook until the liquid is reduced. Add the vegetable stock and seasoning and cook the sauce for 5 minutes. Purée it in a liquidizer, return it to the pan and whisk in the butter in small cubes. Adjust the seasoning if necessary.

Prepare the profiteroles: in a saucepan bring to the boil the water, butter, sugar and salt. Add the flour off the heat, and beat the dough with a wooden spoon until it is smooth. Return the dough to a moderately high heat and cook it for a couple of minutes, stirring constantly. Allow it to cool slightly, then beat in the 3 eggs one at a time.

Butter and flour a baking sheet. Place heaped teaspoons of the dough 2 in/5 cm apart. Add a few drops of water to the beaten egg, and very lightly glaze the surface of each choux puff with the flat edge of the brush. Preheat the oven to 200°C/400°F/Gas 6 and bake for 10 minutes. Reduce the oven to 160°C/325°F/Gas 3 and bake them for another 20 minutes until they are golden.

Instantly slice the tops off the choux puffs to prevent them becoming soggy, scoop out and discard the uncooked inside and cool them on a rack.

Prepare the goat's cheese and leek filling. Cut the roots off the leeks and slice them again where the shoots become a dark green. Slit each leek vertically from the top to half-way down, and wash between the leaves. Halve the leeks vertically and finely slice them. Melt the butter in a saucepan and sweat the leeks for 10 minutes. Add the white wine to the pan and cook this off.

In another small saucepan heat and blend the cream with the goat's cheese and mustard. Add the leeks and the pine nuts to the sauce and adjust the seasoning. The recipe can be prepared to this point ahead of time.

Fill the profiteroles with the goat's cheese and leek mixture, allowing 3 per person. Reheat them in a low oven for a few minutes. Depending on the size of the baby leeks, they may need to be cut into strips. Blanch them in boiling salted water for 2 minutes and drain them. If the red pepper sauce has cooled, warm it through. Pour the sauce on to 6 heated plates, place 3 profiteroles in the centre of each plate, and scatter a few baby leeks over the sauce.

Tomato and Potato Gratin

The use of a good Provençal olive oil in this gratin elevates it to a 'moreish' commodity.

1½ lb/675 g floury potatoes	3 cloves garlic
1 lb/450 g marmande tomatoes	olive oil
6 oz/170 g onions	salt and pepper

Preheat the oven to 170°C/325°F/Gas 3. Scrub the potatoes, then slice them finely using a mandolin or the slicing attachment of a food processor. Peel the tomatoes, and slice them thinly. Peel and halve the onion and cut it into thin slices also. Peel the garlic cloves and cut them into thin slivers.

Brush a gratin dish with olive oil. Make a layer each of potatoes, tomatoes and onions. Season with salt and pepper and dribble some olive oil over. Tuck a few slivers of garlic in here and there. Repeat the layers so that there are three layers of potato and two of tomato, ending with a potato layer. Dribble some olive oil on top of the gratin, season, cover with foil and bake for 30 minutes. Remove the foil, turn the oven up high and cook for another 20 minutes, by which time the top layer should be brown and crisp; if necessary give it a helping hand under the grill.

Iced Mango Parfait

A parfait, which does not require churning while freezing, is the solution to producing high-quality home-made ice-cream if you do not possess an ice-cream machine. The problem of domestic ice-cream machines has never been resolved to the consumer's satisfaction. The best machines have a built-in refrigerator that chills the ice-cream as it churns it. These still seem to be the domain of the professional kitchen. They are large, heavy and expensive. A number of domestic machines built on the same principle are coming on the market, but you would still have to eat a fair deal of ice-cream to justify buying one. The machines at the lower end of the market generally involve either having to freeze the bowl, or a paddle, both of which require forethought and freezer space. They do not lend themselves to the ergonomic lifestyle of an urban dweller who is reliant on a small ice-box at the top of the fridge.

This parfait is delicate and aromatic. It does not require any embellishment or accompanying sauce. At most it could be eaten with almond biscuits (see p. 193). Serve it on a chilled plate dusted with icing sugar, either in thin slices or scoops, depending on what tin you make it in. A parfait tin is cyindrical with one slightly rounded end. If freezer space is limited, a loaf tin or terrine tin offer the most practical option. The parfait could also be set in individual dariole moulds.

7 oz/200 g caster sugar *8 egg yolks*	*1½ large mangoes, or 2 small* * ones* *7 fl oz/200 ml double cream*

Heat the sugar with 4 tablespoons of water to 115°C/230°F. Be careful not to heat the sugar beyond this temperature. Have the egg yolks ready in the bowl of a food processor, pour the boiling syrup over them a little at a time, whisking at a high speed, and continue whisking them at this speed for 4 minutes.

Place the mango flesh in a liquidizer and purée it with some of the egg mixture. Mix together the mango and the rest of the egg mixture in a bowl. If it is still warm, allow it to cool to room temperature.

Whip the cream until it is stiff, and blend it into the mango custard. Pour the mixture into the chosen mould, cover it and freeze it overnight. To unmould the parfait, run a knife around the edge of the mould, invert it, and give it several sharp bangs on the work-surface until it comes out. If it is stubborn, either run the base of the mould over a gas flame or plunge it momentarily into hot water.

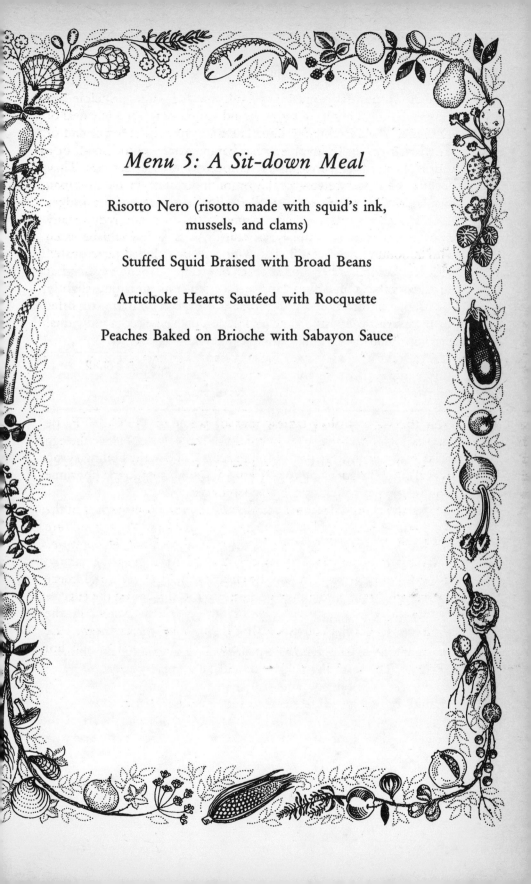

Menu 5: A Sit-down Meal

Risotto Nero (risotto made with squid's ink, mussels, and clams)

Stuffed Squid Braised with Broad Beans

Artichoke Hearts Sautéed with Rocquette

Peaches Baked on Brioche with Sabayon Sauce

Risotto Nero

Dishes of black rice like Risotto Nero are native to Spain and Italy.
The black colouring comes from the ink from squid or cuttlefish.
The ink-sac protects the squid from aggressors; if it feels threatened
it squirts into the water a thin stream of this concentrated ink, which
disperses into a dark murky cloud, confusing its enemy while it
escapes. The ink also imparts a particular, elusive flavour to the
risotto. To obtain a truly black risotto, it is worth extracting the
ink-sacs from more squid than you will be using for the stuffed
squid, keeping the flesh for another recipe. (Try squid rings, lightly
dredged in seasoned flour and deep-fried, served with a glass of
pastis, guaranteed to recall memories for anyone who has sojourned
in the Greek islands.)

There is a theory that squid caught and consumed along the
Mediterranean coast have fuller ink-sacs than the squid on sale in
this country because they are caught using live bait, a method
known as 'jigging', rather than brought in by one of the large
beamers. These beamers churn the catch in such a fashion that much
of the ink is lost by the time the squid is pulled in. At least, so the
theory runs.

The preparation of fish stock does not constitute culinary pleasure for me. Heaving a bag of fish carcasses back home, grisly when
unpacked; the necessity to dispose of them as quickly as possible
once used, and the cleaning up afterwards, all make the operation a
bore. On occasions it is possible to buy prepared fresh stocks – a joy
to stumble across. I hope these become ubiquitous in the future;
stock cubes are no substitute for fresh stocks. If you are preparing a
stock for a recipe, make a large quantity, reduce the excess to double
strength, and freeze it. (See p. 14 for a fish stock recipe.)

The risotto should be made with Italian arborio rice. The
principle is for the rice to absorb a small quantity of simmering
broth at a time. Cooked over a medium heat, it should take about 30
minutes. The resulting risotto should be a creamy mass of grains,
cooked on the outside and still firm to the bite inside. The pan
should be removed from the heat just before it is the right
consistency, for by the time it is served it will have absorbed the
extra liquid. A knob of butter is added to the rice just before serving.

PREPARATION OF SQUID

Jane Grigson described a large block of frozen squid as 'looking like a compressed Last Judgement'. Not a pretty beast, nor especially pleasant to clean, but having mastered the art it is a fast and simple process.

To separate the head from the body, firmly tug the two apart. Remove the hard transparent pen from the body, and the thin porphyry-coloured film which covers it. Wash the pouch well inside and out, removing any remaining substances within.

Cut the tentacles from the head above the eyes, taking care to remove the beak, and reserve them. Attached to the remaining entrails is the ink-sac, visible as a dark line. Snip this at either end with a small pair of scissors, into a bowl. Discard the entrails.

PREPARATION OF MUSSELS AND CLAMS

Scrub the mussels under a running tap, removing barnacles and pulling off the beard with which they secure themselves to an object. Discard any that are broken or do not close when tapped with a knife. Soak the mussels in several changes of cold water for ½-1 hour.

The mussels can be cooked by steaming them open over a high heat in a covered pan. Do not overcrowd the pan, and shake or stir occasionally to circulate the shellfish. Discard any mussels which have not opened. For some sauces the mussels can be cooked with a mirepoix (a mixture of diced carrot, onion, celery and leek), some herbs and white wine. Any resulting liquor should be strained through a sieve lined with kitchen paper or muslin. Depending on the sauce, it may require reducing. Never add any salt to a sauce if you are using mussel liquor, and add the liquor to the basis of the sauce a little at a time to taste, rather than by the measure.

Clams should be prepared like mussels. They retain more sand than mussels, so the soaking is important. Clams can be stubborn in opening and may require longer to steam than mussels. If the clams are large, remove the unopened ones to a separate pan and continue to steam.

Shellfish bought from a fishmonger will have spent a cleansing period in a sterilized seawater tank before it arrives on the slab; and a bona fide supplier will have the tanks checked regularly for the presence of bacteria. Unfortunately a virus will not show up in tests, which means that there is always a risk associated with eating shellfish. Oysters seem to be the highest risk shellfish. I would wager, though, that the chances of acquiring food poisoning from some other source of food probably now outweigh the odds of catching it from shellfish. But it is as well to be aware that there is a small risk attached to eating shellfish, no matter how much care has been taken in the storage, handling and preparation of it.

2 lb/0.9 kg mussels	*10 oz/285 g arborio rice*
1 lb/450 g Venus clams	*5 fl oz/150 ml white wine*
1¾ pint/1 litre fish stock,	*2 tablespoons finely chopped*
including mussel and clam	*Italian parsley*
liquor	*ink-sacs from 2 lb/0.9 kg squid*
2½ oz/70 g butter	*(see above)*
2 oz/55 g shallot	*salt*

Clean and cook the mussels and clams as directed above. Steam them open in a dry pan, and filter the resulting liquor. Add this to the fish stock, making it up to 1¾ pints/1 litre in all. Reserve some mussels for garnish, remove the rest from their shells and set them aside. Leave the clams in their shells.

Heat the fish stock and keep it simmering on the hob. Melt 2 oz/55 g of butter in a large, heavy-bottomed saucepan. Finely chop the shallots, and sweat them in the butter until they are translucent and soft. Add the rice and cook for a couple of minutes. Pour in the wine and simmer until it has been absorbed by the rice. Add half the parsley.

Crush the ink-sacs with a tablespoon of stock in a small bowl. Sieve the ink through a tea-strainer into the risotto, crushing the sacs well with a teaspoon. Return the ink-sacs to the bowl and repeat the process several times until all the ink has been extracted. Start adding the simmering fish stock to the rice, a ladleful at a time so that it is just covered but never flooded.

When the risotto is cooked (about 30 minutes), season it with salt if necessary. Add the shelled mussels to heat through. Stir in half the remaining parsley and the butter. Reheat the reserved mussels and clams for a couple of minutes in a saucepan with a little stock. Use them to garnish the risotto, and sprinkle over the rest of the parsley.

Stuffed Squid Braised with Broad Beans

If squid is cooked briefly, deep-fried in flour, or in and out of a cooking liquid, it will be tender. After a couple of minutes of cooking it toughens up again and must be braised for 30-40 minutes to regain its tenderness.

Squid with body pouches 6 in/15 cm long are required here. The small squid are too delicate and would burst as they cooked. This dish can be cooked either in a covered saucepan or casserole on top of the stove over a low heat, or in a medium hot oven.

1½ lb/675 g young broad beans (frozen ones can be used)	8 tablespoons white wine
6 squid, 6-8 in/15-20 cm long	3 tablespoons fish stock (or white wine)
olive oil	salt
3 tablespoons brandy	double cream

Stuffing

4 shallots	6 oz/170 g fresh breadcrumbs
2 tablespoons olive oil	1 teaspoon thyme, chopped
2 tinned anchovies	2 teaspoons marjoram, chopped
squid tentacles	salt and cayenne pepper

Skin the broad beans and put them to one side.

Prepare the squid as described in the previous recipe. Now prepare the stuffing. Finely chop the shallots, heat the olive oil in a frying-pan, and sweat the shallots until they are soft and translucent. Add the anchovies and crush them until they dissolve. Chop the tentacles, add them to the pan and cook them for a moment. Add the breadcrumbs and herbs, and season the stuffing with salt if necessary, and a pinch of cayenne pepper. Cook the stuffing for a minute or two to allow the flavours to amalgamate.

Loosely fill the squid pouches with stuffing so that they are two-thirds full. Secure the opening with a toothpick, or sew it up if you prefer.

Heat a few tablespoons of olive oil in a casserole and cook the squid, turning them, until they turn opaque and the flesh contracts around the stuffing. Heat the brandy in a ladle; it may ignite of its own accord, but if not, light it and pour it little by little over the squid. It is easy to panic at this stage and pour over too much flaming brandy at once. Add the white wine and cover the pan.

Cook for 25 minutes over a low heat, checking occasionally to make sure the liquid has not evaporated. A little more white wine can be added if necessary.

Add the broad beans to the pan with 2-3 tablespoons of fish stock or white wine; season the dish with salt. Cook the squid for a further 20 minutes. Pour a little cream into the pan so that it forms a sauce with the pan juices. Remove the toothpicks or thread from the squid and serve each one on a bed of broad beans with the sauce spooned over.

Artichoke Hearts Sautéed with Rocquette

6 artichokes   olive oil
6 oz/170 g rocquette   salt and pepper
2 cloves garlic, peeled

Turn the artichokes and cook them as described on p. 32. Slice them thinly. Pick over the rocquette, discarding any damaged leaves. Wash it and dry it between layers of kitchen paper or tea-towels. Mince the garlic.

Heat a little olive oil over a high heat. Working with half the ingredients, throw in the garlic and after a few seconds add the artichokes. After a couple of minutes throw in the rocquette and cook it momentarily until it wilts, seasoning it with salt and pepper. Cook the remaining half of the ingredients in the same way.

Peaches Baked on Brioche with Sabayon Sauce

6 slices brioche   2-3 peaches or nectarines
unsalted butter   soft brown sugar

Preheat the oven to its highest setting.

Remove the crusts or sides of the brioche. Butter the slices on both sides and lay them on a baking tray. Thinly slice the peaches into half-moons, slicing from the top to the bottom of the fruit. Lay 3-4 peach slices on each piece of brioche, and sprinkle over a little soft brown sugar and melted butter.

Cook the slices for 10 minutes, basting them with any juices that run out. The outside and underneath of the brioche should be golden and the peach will have cooked to a melting consistency.

Sabayon Sauce

It is important for the egg to cook sufficiently to create a 'stable' sabayon. If the wine is added too quickly, a superficial froth can be whisked up in seconds which rapidly returns to egg yolks and wine on the plate.

---

4 egg yolks   *8 tablespoons dessert wine*
2 tablespoons sugar

While the peach brioches are cooking, prepare the sabayon. Pour ½ in/1.25 cm of water into the lower half of a double boiler, and set it over a gentle heat. In the top half, whisk together the egg yolks and sugar. Place the top half of the boiler over the bottom half and continue whisking for 1-2 minutes to warm the mixture through. Add the wine little by little, whisking continuously, until it is thick and frothy and forms a ribbon. Remove it from the heat.

Place one piece of peach brioche on each plate and spoon over some of the sabayon.

Menu 6: A Sit-down Meal

Buckwheat Crêpes, Onions Braised in Sherry
Vinegar, and Sour Cream

Gratin of Salmon with Sorrel Sauce

Warm Salad of Oyster Mushrooms
and Saffron

Rhubarb Tart

Buckwheat Crêpes, Onions Braised in Sherry Vinegar, and Sour Cream

Leningrad is a haunting and beautiful city which I had the good fortune to visit some years ago, before Perestroika. The immediate impression on a visitor from the West is the absence of consumer scars: no neon lights, no posters, the exteriors of the buildings remaining intact, much as they must have been when Peter the Great founded the city. There are no obvious signs of the shops, restaurants or markets that feature in European cities. A number of people entering and leaving a building is a possible indicator to a shop or café, but there is unlikely to be any sign or shopfront to advertise it. There were certainly no restaurants. Cafés had on offer a cloying sweet coffee, white or none at all, and some oversweet, dry pastries. Food shops were pitiful — for example, a grocer standing behind his till, the shelves behind him displaying five different cans of food, and vodka.

Let down by my non-existent Russian, I found myself one day standing in a small suburban square on the outskirts of the city instead of at the Hermitage. Across the square people were coming and going from a hangar-like building. Inside there was a fruit and vegetable market, incongruous in this frozen place. Apart from stalls selling root vegetables, there were ton upon ton of apples. A walk around the aisles took me past one stall after another piled high with the same apples — not the perfect ones you expect to find in supermarkets here, but a warts-and-all selection scooped straight from the orchard floor. People queued to fill up their bags. It was the only fruit for sale, and the only fruit to appear at the dinner table.

It goes without saying that there were no feasts of blinis, though caviar and vodka were very evident to the tourist with hard currency. The fact remains that blinis are traditional to Russia, and I hope they feature on the menu of any restaurants that might have opened since Perestroika. A blini is a light, yeasted pancake made with a combination of wheat flour and buckwheat flour. Traditionally blinis are served with sour cream, butter and smoked fish or caviar, washed down with vodka. It is the inclusion of buckwheat and yeast that gives them their quintessential character.

Cocktail-size blinis can be churned out with relative speed, in quantity, and provide a good alternative to pastry or bread-based canapés.

Buckwheat Crêpes

(makes about 24)

4 oz/115 g buckwheat flour	1 sachet dried yeast
4 oz/115 g strong, plain white	½ pint/300 ml milk
flour	¼ pint/150 ml sour cream
½ teaspoon salt	3 eggs, separated
½ teaspoon sugar	1½ oz/45 g melted butter

To serve

10 fl oz/275 ml sour cream

Mix together the flours, salt, sugar and yeast in a large mixing bowl. Heat the milk to blood temperature or slightly warmer, and combine it with the dry ingredients to form a smooth batter. Cover the bowl and place it in a warm place for 1-1½ hours, or until the batter doubles in volume. If the room is cold, warm the oven at its lowest setting for 10 minutes, turn it off, and prove the batter inside it. The batter should not be proved for longer than necessary, or it will become acidic.

Beat the batter well. Add the sour cream, egg yolks and melted butter. Cover the batter again and leave it for 30 minutes in a warm place.

Beat the batter again. Stiffly whip the egg whites and fold them into the batter. Allow it to stand for 10-15 minutes.

The inclusion of melted butter prevents the crêpes from sticking in the pan. The pan may require an initial brushing with a tasteless oil, but no further butter or oil will be required. Heat the pan and drop a small ladle of batter into it so that it spreads to a pancake 3-4 in/7-10 cm in diameter. When the top side appears to dry out and becomes pitted, turn it. Having two frying-pans on the go will halve the cooking time. The crêpes are best eaten hot, straight from the pan, but they can be kept warm, stacked on a plate and covered with foil, or rewarmed like this in a low oven.

Serve them with the braised onions and sour cream.

Onions Braised in Sherry Vinegar

This is Michel Guérard's famous *marmelade d'oignons* from his book *Cuisine Minceur*, borrowed and reinterpreted in how many hundreds of ways.

1¹/₂ lb/675 g onions	1 teaspoon salt
1 teaspoon olive oil	¹/₈ teaspoon pepper
2 teaspoons sugar	3 tablespoons sherry vinegar

Peel the onions, quarter them and slice them thinly. Heat the olive oil in a saucepan, and add the onions, sugar, salt and pepper. Cook, covered, for 35 minutes, letting the onions colour slightly and stirring as needed with a wooden spoon. Then add the vinegar and cook for another 35 minutes over a low heat, still covered and stirring occasionally. The onions should reduce gently throughout the cooking, without sticking, to achieve the desired *marmelade*. Should any liquid remain, cook the onions uncovered for a few minutes until it evaporates.

Serve the *marmelade* warm, with the crêpes and sour cream.

Gratin of Salmon with Sorrel Sauce

Sauce

This is a thin sauce. The fish stock should be reduced to about a quarter of its original volume.

5 fl oz/150 ml vermouth	5 fl oz/150 ml reduced fish stock
2 handfuls sorrel	(or to taste)
8 fl oz/225 ml double cream	salt

Reduce the vermouth by half in a small saucepan. Coarsely chop the sorrel, add it to the pan and cook it until it changes to a dull green. Add the cream and cook the sauce for a few minutes until it thickens. Add fish stock to taste, up to 5 fl oz/150 ml. Purée the sauce in a liquidizer. Season it with salt.

Croûtons

1 small loaf French bread	1¹/₂ oz/45 g butter

Slice the French bread thinly. Lay these croûtons on a baking sheet and place them in a medium hot oven until they dry out and start to change colour. Melt the butter, paint each side of the croûtons, and return them to the oven until they are a golden brown.

Gratin

1 lb/450 g salmon, filleted	*6 oz/170 g fresh young spinach*
1 oz/30 g butter	*leaves*
2 spring onions	*4 eggs*
1 oz/30 g watercress	*¾ pint/450 ml double cream*
	salt and pepper

Enclose the salmon in foil with half the butter, and bake it for 15-20 minutes at 170°C/325°F/Gas 3; it should be cooked to the point where it will flake, though it will still be undercooked. Coarsely chop the onions and watercress. Heat the remaining butter in a frying-pan and sweat the onions and watercress until they appear limp. Wash and pick over the spinach leaves, discarding any stalks. Dry them well and cut the leaves into thin strips. Place the vegetables together in a bowl.

Flake the salmon into the bowl with the vegetables, reserving the cooking juices. Beat the eggs and cream together, add the salmon juices, and combine with the fish and vegetables. Season the mixture and pour it into a buttered gratin dish. Bake for 20-25 minutes at 200°C/400°F/Gas 6. It should still be runny in the centre when it is removed from the oven.

Serve the gratin with the sauce poured over it, accompanied by the croûtons.

Warm Salad of Oyster Mushrooms and Saffron

Garlic vinaigrette

½ small clove garlic	*1 dessertspoon sherry vinegar*
⅓ teaspoon salt	*9 dessertspoons olive oil*

Salad

4 oz/115 g lettuce (mâche and	
one other green variety)	
½ oz/15 g butter	*4 tablespoons white wine*
1 tablespoon olive oil	*1 large pinch saffron filaments*
6 oz/170 g oyster mushrooms	*salt and pepper*

First prepare the vinaigrette. Crush the garlic with the salt until it is reduced to a paste. Whisk this together with the vinegar, then whisk in the olive oil.

Pick over the lettuce, and wash and dry it well.

Heat some of the butter and olive oil in a frying-pan, and cook a single layer of mushrooms at a time, turning them when the underside starts to brown – this happens surprisingly fast.

Toss the salad greens with the vinaigrette in a bowl, and place them on a platter. Scatter the mushrooms over. Deglaze the pan with the white wine. Add the saffron filaments to the pan, season the juice, and simmer for a couple of minutes until the saffron releases its colouring and flavour and the wine is reduced by half. Pour this juice over the salad, and serve it immediately.

Rhubarb Tart

Pastry

5 oz/140 g plain flour	1 egg yolk
1 teaspoon orange zest	1 teaspoon brandy
2 oz/55 g caster sugar	fresh orange juice
3 oz/85 g unsalted butter	

Filling

2 pieces preserved ginger	2 oz/55 g apricot jam, sieved
2 lb/0.9 kg rhubarb	1/2 pint/300 ml double cream
6 tablespoons ginger syrup	large pinch ground cloves
2 oz/55 g sugar	

To make the pastry, place the flour, orange zest, sugar and butter together in the bowl of a food processor, and process to crumbs. Add the egg yolk and brandy, and enough orange juice to bring the pastry together into a ball. Butter and flour a shallow-sided 9-in/23-cm tart tin, press the pastry into it and chill it for 1 hour.

Finely chop the ginger. Wash and trim the rhubarb, cut it into 1-in/2.5-cm lengths and place it in a pan with 4 tablespoons of water, the chopped ginger, ginger syrup and sugar. Cover the pan and simmer the rhubarb until it collapses. Simmer the fruit un-covered until no juice remains. Cool the purée.

Line the pastry case with foil and baking beans, taking care to secure the sides of the case to the tin. Bake for 10 minutes at 180°C/350°F/Gas 4 until the pastry has set. Remove the foil and beans and return the case to the oven for a further 5 minutes until it browns, keeping a careful eye on it. When the case has cooled, warm the apricot jam and paint the base and sides of the pastry. Allow this to set.

Whip the cream with the ground cloves. Spread the base of the tart with the rhubarb purée, and spread the cream over this. Chill the tart until you are ready to serve it. It is best eaten on the day it is made.

Summer

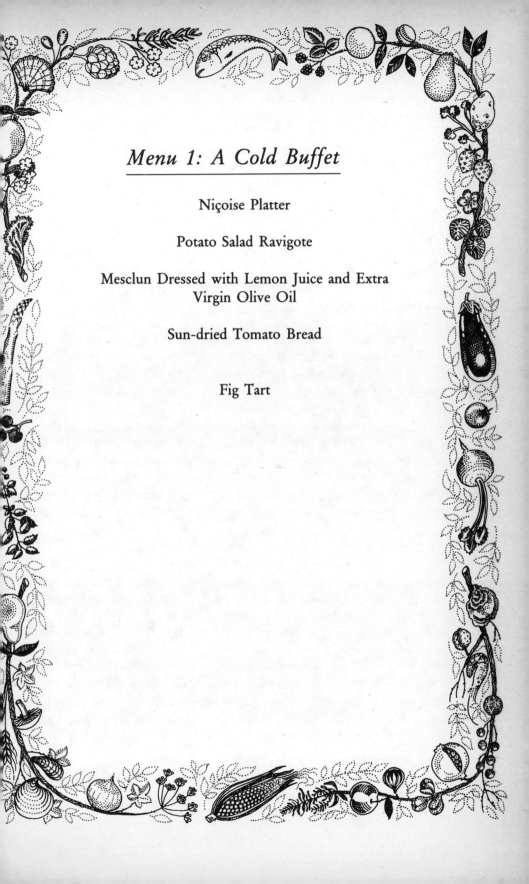

Menu 1: A Cold Buffet

Niçoise Platter

Potato Salad Ravigote

Mesclun Dressed with Lemon Juice and Extra
Virgin Olive Oil

Sun-dried Tomato Bread

Fig Tart

The Niçoise salad as adopted and reinterpreted by the English has come to signify limp green lettuce, hard-boiled eggs, tasteless tomatoes, tinned tuna, a clutch of token olives and anchovies, all awash with a tart dressing. Unforgettable in its own right.

A true Salade Niçoise is composed of ingredients indigenous to Provence, arranged separately on a plate. Fresh tuna is used for this recipe, and it is briefly char-grilled on each side, leaving it still raw in the centre. Cooked in this fashion it remains moist and tender, with all the flavour of char-grilled fish. It is then marinated in olive oil, with garlic and chillies, and the oil is subsequently used to make the dresing. Blue-fin or yellow-fin tuna may be available; the blue-fin, which is the native inhabitant of the Mediterranean, has a richer, darker flesh than the yellow-fin. Currently, however, there is more yellow-fin around. The quail's eggs are boiled just long enough to set the outside of the yolk. The tomatoes should be sweet and ripe, the olives small, wrinkled, salty and strong. Use anchovies preserved in salt should you have access to them, otherwise use a good tinned anchovy — these vary enormously depending on the brand and it is worth working through a number of brands to find a really good one. Poor anchovies are quite detrimental to a dish.

The potato salad is flavoured with mustard, capers and Provençal herbs. Ideally it should be made with summer savory. This uncommon herb is to thyme what chervil is to tarragon. It has undertones of the stronger herb but will not overpower the dish. This is a herb to be kept in a pot on the windowsill. Though quite hardy, it is rarely, if ever, to be found for sale. Summer savory is an annual herb, often known as the 'bean herb' because of its affinity with beans. Winter savory is an evergreen; it has coarser leaves, and thrives in poor soil in sunshine. Savory was once native to this land, having been introduced by the Romans, and both savories were included in John Josslyn's list of plants to be grown in the New American Colonies, to remind settlers of home. It was used like parsley to garnish dishes. It is sad that it should have become so rare today.

Mesclun, which has its home in Southern France (see p. 34), is dressed with the best olive oil interrupted only by a squeeze of lemon juice. This is followed by a tart of fresh figs arranged on an almond custard.

Niçoise Platter

1½ lb/675 g fresh tuna, in steaks ½-¾ in/1.25-2 cm thick	4 oz/115 g thin green beans
extra virgin olive oil	4 oz/115 g radishes
salt and pepper	8 oz/225 g plum tomatoes
4 small cloves garlic	6 anchovies
3 red chillies	1 dessertspoon sherry vinegar
1 dozen quail's eggs	1 oz/30 g rocquette
6-8 baby artichokes, or 4 large artichokes	4 oz/115 g Niçoise olives

Remove the skin, central bone and any inner membranes from the tuna. Brush each side with olive oil and season the steaks with salt and pepper. Heat the griddle very hot, and grill the steaks for 1-2 minutes on each side, so that the outside is charred and the inside is still raw. Finely chop the garlic, halve the chillies discarding any loose seeds, and place these in a shallow container that will hold the steaks in a single layer. Pour in enough extra virgin olive oil to cover the steaks and put the tuna in. Leave to marinate for several hours.

Boil the quail's eggs for 2½ minutes and shell them when they are cool. Once shelled, they can be immersed in cold water in a bowl until they are required.

Turn the artichokes according to the instructions on p. 32, and cook them for 8 minutes if they are baby ones or 15-20 minutes if they are large. Remove the heads from the beans and boil them for 2-3 minutes leaving them firm to the bite.

Quarter the radishes. If you can, use ones with their leaves attached, and remove all the greenery save the last ¼ in/0.75 cm of stalk. Slice the plum tomatoes thickly.

If the anchovies have been preserved in salt, soak them in milk for ½ hour.

Prepare a vinaigrette using garlic and oil from the marinade. Crush ½ teaspoon of the chopped garlic, whisk it together with the sherry vinegar and ½ teaspoon of salt, and add 8 dessertspoons of olive oil.

Strew the rocquette over the base of the platter, reserving a few leaves to tuck between the ingredients once the salad is composed. Break the tuna into pieces and place it in the centre. Arrange the remaining salad components separately around the tuna, alternating the colours. Whisk the vinaigrette and pour it over the salad.

Potato Salad Ravigote

A *sauce ravigote* is highly flavoured, and has any number of interpretations. This version is a mayonnaise flavoured with capers, mustard and a group of herbs redolent of Provence.

Mayonnaise

2 egg yolks	1/2 pint/300 ml pure olive oil
1/2 teaspoon mustard	squeeze of lemon juice
1/4 teaspoon salt	

Potatoes

3 tablespoons of watercress, summer savory, chives, parsley and chervil	1 tablespoon capers
	1 1/2 lb/675 g new potatoes

Prepare the mayonnaise by whisking together the egg yolks, mustard and salt. Continue whisking while adding the olive oil in a thin stream. When the mayonnaise is too thick and the egg yolk has become saturated with oil, thin it to the correct consistency with cold water. Add the water with discretion — too much water will reduce the richness of the mayonnaise. Squeeze in a touch of lemon juice.

Finely chop the watercress and herbs, reserving some chervil fronds as a garnish. Add them and the capers, coarsely chopped, to the mayonnaise. Adjust the seasoning. The sauce benefits from standing for a few hours for the flavours to develop.

Scrub the potatoes and boil them for 10-15 minutes. When they are cool, cut them into pieces or slice them thickly. Place them on a plate, spoon the mayonnaise over and garnish with the chervil fronds.

Mesclun Dressed with Lemon Juice and Extra Virgin Olive Oil

For mesclun, see p. 34. Toss it in a bowl with your finest olive oil, preferably one from Provence, and season it with salt and pepper. Squeeze a hint of lemon juice over the salad.

Fig Tart

Most fruit tarts are best served freshly assembled, as soon as the glaze has set. It is hard to prevent juices from seeping down to the pastry after a few hours, often reducing it to a soggy mess. Figs, however, are a comparatively dry fruit and this seepage is not such a problem, though the figs do discolour a little in due course.

Pastry

5 oz/140 g plain flour	3 oz/85 g unsalted butter
2 oz/55 g caster sugar	1 egg yolk
	orange juice

Frangipan

1 egg	½ pint/300 ml milk
1 egg yolk	1½ oz/45 g unsalted butter
4 oz/115 g caster sugar	½ teaspoon vanilla essence
2 oz/55 g plain flour	3 oz/85 g ground almonds

To assemble

10 figs	3 oz/85 g apricot jam

To serve

crème fraîche

To make the pastry, place the flour and sugar in the bowl of a food processor, add the butter and reduce the mixture to crumbs. Add the egg yolk, and bring it all together with orange juice. Butter and flour a 9-in/23-cm tart tin, press the pastry into it and chill it for 1 hour. Line the case with foil and baking beans, firmly securing the sides of the case to the sides of the tin. Bake the case for 10 minutes at 180°C/350°F/Gas 4 until the pastry has set. Remove the foil and beans and return the case to the oven for another 5 minutes until it is golden. Because of the sugar in the pastry it is cooked to perfection in a fleeting moment, so keep a careful eye on it during the second cooking.

To prepare the frangipan, beat the egg and egg yolk together with the sugar until pale and creamy. Beat in the flour. Heat the milk to boiling point and whisk it into the mixture. Return this to the pan and cook it for 2-3 minutes, stirring constantly as it turns into a thick custard. Beat in the butter, vanilla essence and ground almonds. Remove the custard to a bowl and cool it, covering the surface with cling-film to prevent a skin forming.

To assemble the tart, spread the frangipan on the base of the tart case. Slice the figs vertically and arrange them so that they overlap, working outwards, until the base is covered. The ends can be used to good effect in the centre of the tart and around the edge.

Heat the apricot jam until it thins, and pass it through a sieve. Glaze the tart and allow it to set. Serve it with *crème fraîche*.

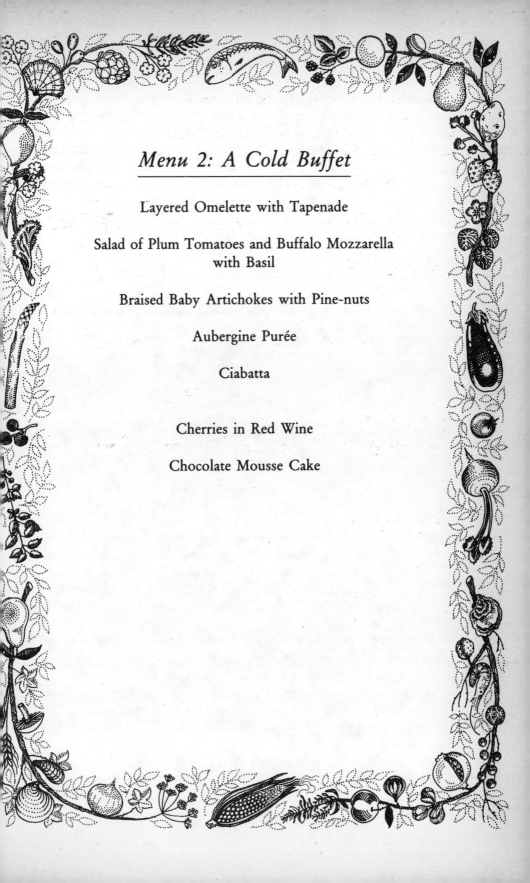

Menu 2: A Cold Buffet

Layered Omelette with Tapenade

Salad of Plum Tomatoes and Buffalo Mozzarella
with Basil

Braised Baby Artichokes with Pine-nuts

Aubergine Purée

Ciabatta

Cherries in Red Wine

Chocolate Mousse Cake

Layered Omelette with Tapenade

This omelette consists of two layers, a green layer of spinach and watercress, and a red pepper layer. It can be eaten hot or cold. As part of a simpler meal it is good served with a plain green salad and some char-grilled toast, doused in olive oil.

Spinach and watercress layer

¾ lb/340 g spinach	salt and pepper
3 oz/85 g watercress	4 eggs
1 clove garlic	4 fl oz/115 ml double cream
1 oz/30 g butter	1 tablespoon freshly grated Parmesan

Red pepper layer

3 red peppers	pinch thyme
2 tablespoons olive oil	salt and pepper
1 tablespoon tomato purée	6 eggs

Tapenade
See recipe on p. 113 – make double quantity.

First, heat the oven to 200°C/400°F/Gas 6 and roast the red peppers according to the instructions on p. 108. Do not overcook them – 20 minutes should be long enough. Turn the oven down to 160°C/300°F/Gas 2.

Wash the spinach and watercress and dry it well. Remove any tough stalks and finely slice the leaves. Mince the garlic. Heat a knob of butter in a frying-pan, and as it foams add a little of the garlic and some of the leaves. Cook them until they wilt. Remove them to a bowl and season them. Cook the remaining leaves in batches, in the same fashion.

In another bowl whisk the eggs. Strain them into the greens, add the cream and Parmesan, and mix well.

Butter an 8-in/20-cm terrine, line the base with baking parchment, and butter this as well. Pour in the mixture. Cover the terrine with foil and stand it in a bain-marie so that the water comes two-thirds of the way up the sides. Bake this layer for 35 minutes or until it sets.

Peel and seed the roasted peppers and pat them dry. Heat the olive oil in a frying-pan and cook the peppers for 5 minutes. Turn them over, add the tomato purée and thyme, and season with salt and pepper. Cook them for another 5 minutes. Reduce the peppers to a coarse purée in a food processor.

Whisk the eggs in a bowl and pass them through a sieve into the pepper purée. Pour this on top of the spinach layer, cover the omelette with greased foil and return it to the oven for 20 minutes, or until it has set.

Unmould the omelette and serve it in slices with the tapenade to the side. Garnish it with a few salad leaves, such as mâche, rocquette or watercress.

Salad of Plum Tomatoes and Buffalo Mozzarella with Basil

Mediterranean plum tomatoes, oblong in shape with a sweet crimson flesh, are a world apart from any other variety. They are the only tomato I enjoy eating whole in the hand as a fruit. Happily most supermarkets and markets stock them over the summer, and it is easy enough to satiate a passion for them during these months.

Genuine buffalo mozzarella, not the ersatz imitation made from cow's milk or a percentage thereof, is of increasing rarity, since buffaloes are in decline. Italian buffalo mozzarella, the type most often found in this country, must by law state what percentage of what milk it contains. So if it proclaims '*prodotta con solo latte di bufala*', buy it.

Compared to the rubbery, bland cow's milk variety, buffalo mozzarella has a sharp taste and a flaky constitution. It tastes delicate yet strong, and the flavour still comes through when married with a slice of tomato or avocado.

Anna Del Conte writes in *Gastronomy of Italy* that buffalo mozzarella should ideally be eaten the day after it is made, 'absolutely fresh and dripping with its own buttermilk'. Such an experience is likely to elude the majority of people all their days, but searching out a packaged cheese made with 100 per cent buffalo milk is a reward in itself.

Mozzarella can be kept in a bowl in the fridge, covered with its whey and some water, for up to 8 days.

Opal basil is a rare but worthy herb. It has porphyry-coloured jagged leaves, and a subtle sweetness which gives it the edge over ordinary green basil. It is well worth growing if you can. Alternatively, elaborate the salad by steeping some olive oil with basil leaves and whole cloves of garlic for a few days and using this as the dressing. This is of perennial use in the kitchen to dress any number of salads, or for use in sauces, or simply as a replacement for butter. Alternatively place some torn basil leaves in a pestle and mortar, cover them with olive oil and crush them.

4 ripe plum tomatoes	a 6 oz/170 g buffalo mozzarella
salt and pepper	olive oil
pinch of sugar	basil, opal or green

Slice the tomatoes, discarding the end slice containing the core. Pile them in circles on a plate, mounding them in the centre. Season the tomato with salt and pepper and sprinkle with a generous pinch of sugar. Allow the salad to stand for 15 minutes for the juices to start running.

Slice the mozzarella and arrange it over the centre of the salad. Dribble some olive oil over. Tear some basil leaves and scatter them over the salad, placing some whole leaves in the centre.

Braised Baby Artichokes with Pine-nuts

If baby artichokes are unavailable, use 8 normal-sized artichokes. Turn them according to the instructions on p. 32. Remove the choke, which rapidly discolours to a dark green on exposure to air. Thinly slice each heart and proceed as below.

3 lb/1.4 kg baby artichokes	12 black peppercorns
(yields 1 lb/450 g hearts)	1/4 teaspoon fennel seeds
4 oz/115 g celery heart	6 coriander seeds
3/4 pint/450 ml water	1 shallot, finely chopped
1/8 pint/75 ml best extra virgin	6 parsley stalks
olive oil	1 1/2 oz/45 g pine-nuts
juice of 1/2 lemon	chervil leaves
1/2 teaspoon salt	

Turn the baby artichokes according to the instructions on p. 32. Remove all the tough outer leaves so that only a small tender bud remains. The choke is edible. Cut the celery into 2-in/5-cm juliennes.

Make an aromatic broth by combining all the remaining ingredients in a pan, except for the pine-nuts and chervil. Contain the seeds in a small piece of muslin. Bring the broth to the boil and simmer for 10 minutes.

Halve each artichoke heart vertically and lay the halves face downwards in the broth; add the celery. Bring the broth back to the boil, cover the pan tightly, turn the heat down low and simmer for 10-12 minutes.

Remove the vegetables to a bowl. Reduce the remaining broth to several tablespoons of liquid. Check the salt. Discard the seeds, strain the reduced liquid over the artichokes and allow them to cool.

Preheat the oven to 170°F/325°C/Gas 3 and toast the pine-nuts for 7-8 minutes on a tray. Just before serving the dish, mix the pine-nuts into the artichokes and add some extra olive oil if it seems appropriate. Arrange the vegetables on a platter and scatter some chervil leaves over.

Aubergine Purée

See p. 114.

Cherries in Red Wine

The oft-maligned marriage of chocolate and cherries has an enduring charm for me. This is a rich combination, pleasantly orchestrated by almond biscuits (see p. 193) and a river of cream. Cherries aside, if death by chocolate were a reality this is how I should like to go. Alternatively, spread a layer of whipped cream and *crème fraîche* on the cake, and some strawberries, raspberries or *fraises des bois* on top.

1½ lb/675 g black cherries	*2-in/5-cm strip of lemon zest*
12 fl oz/325 ml good red wine	*large pinch of cinnamon*
3 oz/85 g caster sugar	*3 oranges*

Pit the cherries. Place the wine, sugar, lemon zest and cinnamon in a saucepan and bring to the boil. Add the cherries, cover the pan and simmer gently for 20 minutes.

Remove the cherries to a bowl, discard the lemon zest and reduce the liquid by half to a syrupy liquor. Pour this over the cherries and allow them to cool before covering them with cling-film and chilling them.

Segment the oranges by cutting off the skin and pith, run a knife between each segment to remove the orange flesh, leaving the pith which separates them. Add these to the cherries.

Chocolate Mousse Cake

This recipe is adapted from *More Gretta Anna Recipes*, a book by an Australian cook who also runs a cookery school in Sydney. Many of my favourite cakes derive from this source.

---

1 lb/450 g bitter chocolate   *4 eggs*
4 oz/115 g unsalted butter   *1 tablespoon flour*
2½ tablespoons caster sugar

Preheat the oven to 200°C/400°F/Gas 6. Melt the chocolate with the butter and 1½ tablespoons of sugar. Whisk the eggs and the remaining sugar together for 5-10 minutes in a food processor until they are doubled in volume, thick, creamy and almost white. Fold the flour into the eggs. Combine the two mixtures as deftly as possible. Do not be alarmed by the liquid nature of the cake mixture at this point; it sets partially when it is cooked and further as it cools.

Butter an 8-in/20-cm springform cake tin. Pour in the chocolate mousse. Cook the cake for 7 minutes. From the rim to ¾ in/2 cm inside should be firm, the centre of the cake still liquid. Cool the cake, cover it and chill it for several hours or overnight.

Remove the cake from the fridge ½ hour before serving it. Remove the springform collar, cut the cake into wedges, and serve with the cherries and some cream.

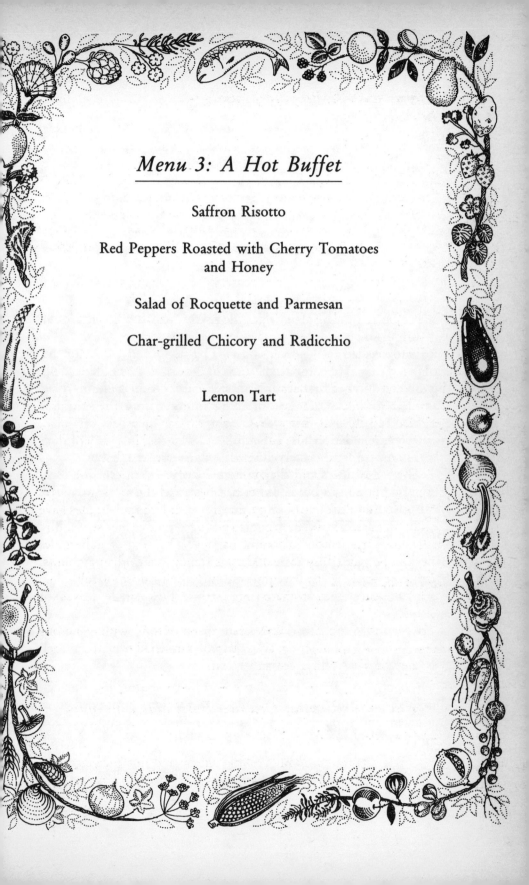

Menu 3: A Hot Buffet

Saffron Risotto

Red Peppers Roasted with Cherry Tomatoes
and Honey

Salad of Rocquette and Parmesan

Char-grilled Chicory and Radicchio

Lemon Tart

Saffron Risotto

Villa Pliniana, on Lake Como, sheltered Anguissola, a small-time tyrant and assassin who once governed Como. He was a good governor but a dubious patriot. After killing a priest in his youth he was banished to Piacenza, where he joined the court of Duke Pier Luigi Farnese; he subsequently betrayed the Duke, who had gained control of Piacenza. Assisting the Emperor and the King of Spain to hand over the city to Ferrante Gonzaga, he stabbed the Duke.

While well rewarded, he wisely fled from Piacenza, and Pliniana became his fortress. The villa, built in the sixteenth century, bears Pliny's name because of his fascination with the spring that runs intermittently from above the house, suddenly ceasing to flow every four hours. A branch of it which flows through the house would chill Anguissola's wine.

Rossini was led to this haunting villa by its solitude, save for the crashing waters. He composed *Tancredi* here, but when the leading lady objected to her first act aria, shortly before it opened, he wrote 'Tanti Palpiti' in the time it took him to eat a Milanese risotto in a trattoria. Henceforth this was known as the 'rice aria' — what greater commendation for a risotto?

If this risotto is to be served on its own, increase the amount by half. The red peppers and char-grilled chicory and radicchio which feature in this menu would need to be cut smaller if this was part of a stand-up buffet.

---

1 small onion	*1¹/₂-2 pints/0.9-1.1 litres light*
2¹/₂ oz/70 g butter	*vegetable stock (a dark-*
10 oz/285 g arborio rice	*coloured stock will produce a*
5 fl oz/150 ml white wine	*dark and murky risotto)*
2 sachets saffron (approx ¹/₄	*2 oz/55 g freshly grated*
teaspoon)	*Parmesan*
	salt
	chopped Italian parsley

Finely chop the onion. Heat 2 oz/55 g of the butter in a heavy-bottomed pan and sweat the onion over a low heat until it is translucent and soft; it must not colour. Add the rice and cook for 1-2 minutes. Pour in the wine and continue to cook until it has been absorbed. Add the saffron and start to pour in ladles of simmering stock — at no stage should the rice be flooded. It will take about

25-30 minutes to cook. Stop cooking the risotto while it is still too moist, and it should then arrive on the table the correct consistency.

Stir in the Parmesan and the remaining ½ oz/15 g of butter. Adjust the seasoning and serve with a light sprinkling of chopped parsley.

Red Peppers Roasted with Cherry Tomatoes and Honey

These peppers are at their best served warm. An attractive arrangement is to use red and yellow peppers and red and yellow cherry tomatoes, creating a harlequin effect.

3 red peppers	olive oil
¾ lb/340 g cherry tomatoes	salt and pepper
3 teaspoons honey	flat-leaf parsley to garnish

Cut the peppers in half from the stem to the base, leaving the green stalk. Remove the seeds and pith. Halve the cherry tomatoes and fill the pepper cavities with these. Dribble over the honey and a little olive oil, season with salt and pepper, and bake them in a very hot oven for 20-30 minutes, until the peppers are wilted and patched with brown. Serve them garnished with the parsley.

As the peppers cook, the juice from the tomatoes combines with the juice from the peppers, merging with the honey and olive oil into a heavenly liquid which demands that a loaf of good bread is at hand.

Salad of Rocquette and Parmesan

The versatility of rocquette as a herb and salad ingredient makes its comeback most desirable. While cultivated since Roman times, and grown by John Evelyn as a salad green, until recently it remained almost obsolete except in the Southern Mediterranean. It grows with proficiency, so there is no reason why it should not soon appear for sale in large bags or bunches, rather than being sold by the leaf in small polystyrene containers, which makes many of the best ways of using it unfeasible.

It has a distinctly strong, peppery flavour, and the leaves are best eaten young and tender, less than 6 in/15 cm long. It thrives in cool sunny weather in a rich soil, so early autumn and spring are good times to feast on it.

This salad can be served as a first course with bruschetta and yellow pear tomatoes; if it is springtime, throw in some lightly steamed sprouting broccoli, or calabrese in the autumn.

I like to have rocquette around as I would watercress. It can garnish or accompany a myriad of little dishes. It is wonderful wilted in olive oil with garlic and tossed into pasta. Or you can make a warm salad of thickly sliced new potatoes, dress them with olive oil, season them and throw in some rocquette, then scatter over a strong cheese, sun-dried tomatoes or anchovies. I have had it as a starter with fresh goat's cheese and figs, also a good combination.

4 oz/115 g rocquette	*olive oil*
3 oz/85 g fresh Parmesan	*salt and pepper*

Pick over the rocquette and wash and dry it well. Thinly slice the Parmesan — use a mandolin if you have one. Toss the rocquette with olive oil and season it. Arrange it on a plate with the thinly sliced Parmesan.

Char-grilled Chicory and Radicchio

1 head radicchio	*olive oil*
3 heads chicory	*salt and pepper*

Remove the outer leaves of the radicchio and chicory. Cut the chicory in half vertically. Cut each radicchio into eighths (more if it is especially large), so that the leaves are held together by the root. If necessary the segments can be secured with a toothpick, which should be removed before it is served. Brush all these segments with olive oil and season them on both sides. Char-grill them and serve them on a platter with more olive oil dribbled over.

Lemon Tart

I harbour a passion for lemon desserts, both ersatz and real; this is possibly the best and most quintessentially 'lemon' dessert I have ever tasted. The pastry case is deeply filled with lemon custard, which when baked at a low temperature becomes a firm, relentlessly citrus, cream. This recipe is based on the lemon tart so often on the menu at Kensington Place, in Notting Hill, London.

Pastry

7 oz/200 g plain flour	1 egg yolk
1 oz/30 g caster sugar	1 teaspoon brandy
3½ oz/100 g butter	iced water

Custard

9 fl oz/250 ml double cream	9 eggs
7 fl oz/200 ml lemon juice and zest of the lemons used (4-5 lemons)	10 oz/285 g caster sugar

First, heat the cream to boiling point, add the lemon zest, and infuse for several hours, or overnight, in a cool place. This is not essential but lends even more 'lemon' to the final product.

Prepare the pastry by placing the flour and sugar in the bowl of a food processor. Add the butter in cubes and process it to crumbs. Add the egg yolk, the brandy and enough iced water to bring the dough together. Reserve a small amount of pastry to patch up any cracks in the shell after baking it blind. Butter and flour an 8-in/20-cm springform tin and press the pastry into it so that the sides are 2 in/5 cm deep. Chill it for 1 hour.

Line the shell with foil and baking beans, securing the pastry sides firmly to the tin. Bake the case for 10 minutes at 180°C/350°F/Gas 4 until it has set. Remove the foil and continue to bake the case for 5-10 minutes, until it is golden and completely cooked. Allow it to cool, then patch any cracks that have appeared with the reserved uncooked pastry.

Whisk together the eggs and sugar. Stir in the lemon juice, zest and cream. Pour this mixture into the pastry shell and bake it at 125°C/225°F/Gas ½ for 1½ hours, until it has set. Check it after ¾ hour to make sure it is starting to set − turn the oven up if it is still a barely warm liquid, and down if it appears to be cooking too quickly. It is important that the tart is removed from the oven as soon as it has set. When it is cooked, chill the tart to larder temperature.

Trim the top of the pastry to be level with the custard while the springform collar is in place. Liberally dust the surface of the tart with icing sugar just before serving it. Serve it with whipped cream or *crème fraîche*.

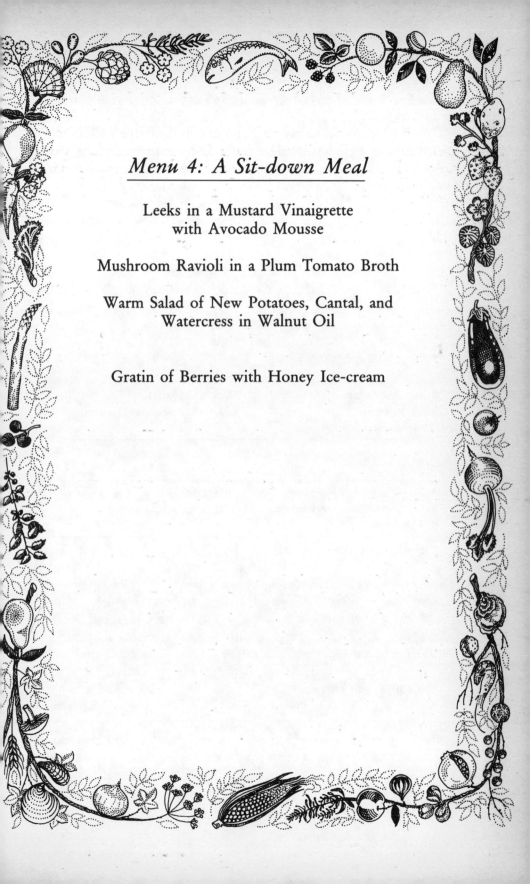

Menu 4: A Sit-down Meal

Leeks in a Mustard Vinaigrette
with Avocado Mousse

Mushroom Ravioli in a Plum Tomato Broth

Warm Salad of New Potatoes, Cantal, and
Watercress in Walnut Oil

Gratin of Berries with Honey Ice-cream

Leeks in a Mustard Vinaigrette with Avocado Mousse

This dish is perhaps best made at the end of the summer when baby leeks are available. If you are using ordinary leeks, use half the amount and halve or quarter them lengthwise after they are cooked. Leeks can be hard to obtain in June, in which case use asparagus, or celery, fennel, courgette or cucumber cut into long juliennes and blanched.

Of the various avocados to be had, go for the small, rough-skinned, dark Hass avocados, which have a rich, compact flesh. Some of the large bright green avocados are lacking in flavour and tend to be watery.

The avocado mousse will need to set for 8 hours or overnight. The dish is quite rich and should be served with bread or toast.

Mousse

6 small avocados, or 3 large ones	2 sachets of gelatine
juice of 1 lemon	½ pint/300 ml double cream
salt and white pepper	

Vinaigrette

6 large leeks, or 12 baby ones	1 heaped teaspoon grain mustard
1½ dessertspoons sherry vinegar	10 dessertspoons olive oil
⅓ teaspoon salt	

Scoop the avocado flesh into the bowl of a food processor, and purée it together with the lemon juice and some salt and pepper. Dissolve the gelatine, thoroughly, in a couple of tablespoons of boiling water. To assist this you can stand the bowl in which you are dissolving the gelatine in a bain-marie, but the gelatine should never be allowed to boil. If it is still only partially dissolved, strain it through a fine mesh sieve. Warm the cream to room temperature and stir a little into the gelatine. If the gelatine solidifies, warm the mixture in a bain-marie or double boiler until it liquefies. Add the remaining cream to the gelatine, combine it with the avocado, and reprocess the purée.

Butter and line a 6-in/15-cm terrine tin with baking parchment paper, so that the paper comes up over the sides of the tin. If your tin is larger than this, you can block off the end with foil or parchment. Spoon the avocado mixture into the tin, cover the surface with the parchment and allow the mousse to set.

Trim the root end of the leeks, and remove the shoots where they turn a dark green. Wash them well and boil them for 15 minutes, until they are completely cooked. Baby leeks, depending on their size, will be cooked more quickly. Drain them, and dry them on kitchen paper.

Make a mustard vinaigrette by whisking together the vinegar, salt and mustard, then adding the olive oil.

To serve the dish, unmould the avocado mousse and cut it into ½-in/1.25-cm slices. Place one or two of these on each plate. Spoon the vinaigrette around the mousse. Cut the leeks lengthwise into either halves or quarters. Put some of these beside the mousse. Grind some white pepper over each plate.

Mushroom Ravioli in a Plum Tomato Broth

I hesitated to take home-made pasta on board for many years. But a lack of excuses to visit Soho and slip into Lina Stores or Fratelli Camisa to buy some of their wonderful filled pastas finally drove me to arm myself with a rolling-pin and a manual and get stuck in.

The commercially produced 'fresh' filled pastas are usually a mass of bland-tasting stodge, with all the effort put into the cosmetic appearance of the product rather than into the filling and the encasing pasta. After the initial fumblings, pasta-making now seems like the simplest of procedures, with the potential for endless creativity; and you can be smug in the knowledge that you really cannot buy anything as delicious as what you are making.

I do not possess a pasta machine. Instead I use a long thin wooden rolling-pin 1½-2 in/4-5 cm thick and about 2½ feet/75 cm long. I have not found it difficult rolling the pasta by hand, so do not feel you must rush out and buy the kit before you start.

Pasta dough

Traditionally the pasta should consist only of flour and eggs, but a tablespoon of milk is added here to facilitate sealing the edges of the ravioli. It is difficult to give exact quantities of flour to eggs, since the size of the eggs and their absorption quality are variable, but the received wisdom seems to be 1 egg (size 2) to 3 oz/85 g of flour. The eggs should be fresh and free range, and the flour should be unbleached strong white. The yellower, hard-wheat or semolina flour is also used in pasta-making, but it has a higher gluten content which does not give the dough the necessary elasticity for a thin hand-rolled pasta.

10½ oz/300 g strong plain white flour	*3 eggs* *1 tablespoon milk*

To avoid an excess of flour, the dough should be prepared by first making a mound of flour on the work surface, with a hollow in the centre. Break the eggs into this, add the milk, and whisk slightly with a fork. Draw the flour into the eggs gradually, working with your hands, until the egg has absorbed as much flour as it can. Now the dough must be kneaded for 8 minutes. I confess to breaking these rules at times and performing the whole operation in the food processor, kneading the dough for 4 minutes; this is definitely not *de rigueur*, and may result in an excess of flour.

Divide the dough into four, and wrap each piece in cling-film. Allow it to rest for 30 minutes.

Filling

¼ oz/10 g dried wild mushrooms	*2 tablespoons chopped flat-leaf*
1 lb/450 g mushrooms	*parsley*
2 shallots	*4 oz/115 g cream cheese*
½ oz/30 g butter	*1 tablespoon freshly grated*
1 tablespoon arachide (ground-	*Parmesan*
nut) oil	*1 egg yolk*
salt and pepper	

Cover the dried mushrooms with boiling water and set them aside to soak for 15 minutes. Wipe the fresh mushrooms. Prepare a mushroom duxelles by finely chopping the fresh mushrooms in a food processor, placing them in a tea-towel and squeezing out all the water. This is essential to the success of the ravioli. A wet filling will ruin the pasta casing.

Finely chop the shallots. Heat the butter and oil in a frying-pan. Add the shallots and mushroom duxelles together to the pan and cook them for 7-8 minutes until the mushrooms start to colour and separate into individual pieces. Season well, and add the parsley. Drain the dried mushrooms, and dry them on kitchen paper. Finely chop them and add them to the mushroom duxelles together with the cream cheese, Parmesan and egg yolk.

Place a quarter of the pasta dough on a lightly floured work surface. Dust the rolling-pin with flour. Start to roll the dough, rotating it as you go, stretching the dough outwards with the rolling-pin. Apply only light pressure to the rolling-pin, concentrating on pushing it away from you. This motion is different from the way in which pastry is rolled, where a downward pressure is applied to stretch the dough.

Roll the dough as thinly as possible – it should have the appearance of thin parchment. Place ¼ teaspoons of the filling on the sheet of dough in a column, with 1 in/2.5 cm between each mound. Fold the far edge of the pasta over the row of filling to form a tube. Trim along the tube with a pastry cutter and cut between the mounds of filling to form ravioli. Press the edges of the ravioli firmly together. Continue with the rest of the sheet, then proceed with the remaining pieces of dough. To make larger ravioli, simply use more filling and space it further apart on the sheet of dough. Should you find that the edges will not adhere because the dough has become too dry, moisten them with a little milk.

Lay the ravioli out on a tea-towel and dry them a little on both sides if they are not to be used immediately. Dust them with semolina, and store them between layers of greaseproof paper until you are ready to cook them.

To cook the pasta, bring a large pan of water to the boil and add a tablespoon of olive oil and a generous pinch of salt. Add the ravioli and boil gently till they are cooked but not overdone – this point is easily missed with home-made pasta. If the pasta are cooked as soon as they are made they may take as little as 2 minutes; otherwise, depending on how dry they are, it will take longer.

Broth

2 shallots	2 tablespoons olive oil
2 lbs/0.9 kg plum tomatoes	salt and pepper

Garnish

chervil leaves

Finely chop the shallots and slice the tomatoes. Heat the olive oil in a saucepan and sweat the shallots for 2-3 minutes. Add the tomatoes, cover the pan, turn the heat down very low and cook the sauce for 45 minutes, stirring occasionally, until the tomatoes collapse. Liquidize the contents of the pan and pass them through a sieve, reserving the broth. Season with salt and pepper.

Serve the ravioli with the broth poured over them. Scatter plenty of chervil leaves over the dish. If chervil is unavailable, then finely chopped parsley, chives and a hint of tarragon can replace it.

Warm Salad of New Potatoes, Cantal, and Watercress in Walnut Oil

Cantal is a hard-pressed, high-fat cheese from the Cantal mountains in the Auvergne region of France. It is thought to be the ancestor of French cheeses, being mentioned in Roman scriptures. It bears marked similarities to Cheddar, and the technique of making it may have been introduced to this country by the Romans. Cantal is a fabulous cheese, with a strong nutty flavour. It is softer than Cheddar, and while it has the same fat content it tastes richer.

Cantal carries an *appellation d'origine* label; it is produced either on small mountain farms or in dairies, the product of the former being the finer. The best milk comes from the summer pastures. Cantal can be eaten young, ageing or old; mature Cantal is quite sour and dry, and I prefer a younger one. If you cannot get it, use a good mature Cheddar.

1½ oz/45 g watercress	*walnut oil*
6 oz/170 g Cantal	*salt and pepper*
1 lb/450 g new potatoes	

Pick over the watercress, wash and dry it well and place it in a salad bowl. Break the Cantal into ½-in/1.25-cm cubes. Scrub the potatoes and boil them for 10 minutes (depending on their size — they should be just cooked).

Break the potatoes in half and toss them with plenty of walnut oil, salt and pepper in another bowl. Toss these into the watercress and scatter over the cubed Cantal.

Gratin of Berries

Berries which immediately spring to mind and could be included here are loganberries, raspberries, strawberries, blueberries, *fraises des bois*, blackberries, redcurrants and blackcurrants. Certainly a mixture of black and red berries looks extremely attractive, and the addition of some currants gives it an added dimension. Should you be a keen gardener, or be related to one, you may have access to some of the more unusual berries to be had. Jostaberries, Japanese wineberries, boysenberries, silvanberries, veitchberries and white currants all have a gardener's ring to their name.

The custard used here is a crème patissière with the addition of whipped egg whites. It could also be made with zabaglione, which would be considerably richer and would require more last-minute attention.

---

generous ½ pint/300 ml milk	½ oz/15 g butter
zest of ½ orange	2 egg whites
3 egg yolks	1¼ lb/565 g berries
4½ oz/125 g caster sugar	icing sugar
½ oz/15 g flour	

Prepare the custard. Bring the milk to the boil, add the orange zest and infuse it for 15 minutes. Whisk the egg yolks and caster sugar together until they are pale, then incorporate the flour. Strain the milk and smooth a little of it into the paste, and then the rest. Return the custard to the pan and cook it for 2-3 minutes, dispersing any lumps. Beat in the butter. Cover the custard with cling-film and allow it to cool.

Shortly before assembling the gratin, whip the egg whites until they are stiff and add them to the custard.

Spoon the custard over the base of individual plates or two large platters, arrange the fruit on top and press it into the custard. The top of the fruit should show through. Liberally dust the surface with icing sugar and brown it under a hot grill. Serve the gratin with a large scoop of ice-cream.

Honey Ice-cream

This recipe calls for a good aromatic honey. I remain biased in my preference for English honey. The different varieties are evocative of the seasons and areas in which they were produced. It does not take an incurable romantic to be inspired by the idea of sleepy hives of bees waking up with the warm weather, producing different varieties of honey as the seasons progress – feasting on plum blossom and hawthorn one day and on clover and dandelion the next.

A beekeeper leads his bees to the flowers: in Kent the bees will feed on the orchard blossom producing the pale blossom honey, simultaneously pollinating the trees. In Scotland the bees will feast on acres of heather to produce the dark amber heather honey. More often the bees will feed from a variety of flowers and trees to produce a mixed honey. A beekeeper will probably be able to taste a honey and tell what the bees have been feeding from.

Pure honey, untreated, blended or purified, minutes or hours after it has been extracted from the comb, makes a mockery of the major brands. Sadly the harsh winter of 1987 killed many swarms, making it uneconomical for some small producers to continue. Those that remain are most likely to be selling to a small local grocer. Worth picking up a jar or two on the next foray to the countryside.

Basically the ice-cream consists of a crème anglaise sweetened with honey, with the addition of whipped cream. Crème anglaise, whipped cream and flavourings various is a good formula for any home-made ice-cream; but an ice-cream machine is essential for good results. Apart from the expensive machines with an inbuilt motor, they all tend to have drawbacks (see Iced Mango Parfait, p. 51).

---

18 fl oz/500 ml milk	*6 tablespoons honey*
8 egg yolks	*5 fl oz/150 ml double cream*

Bring the milk to the boil in a saucepan. Whisk together the egg yolks and honey. Stir some of the milk into them and return the mixture to the pan. Stir the custard continuously over a low heat until it coats the back of a spoon. Strain it through a sieve. Cover the surface with cling-film and allow it to cool.

Whip the cream and stir it into the custard. Freeze the ice-cream according to the manufacturer's instructions for the machine. The ice-cream will benefit from softening at room temperature for 10 minutes before it is served.

Menu 5: A Barbecue

Char-grilled Fennel with Fresh Herbed Cheese

Salmon Trout Steamed between Wild Grasses,
with Samphire and Horseradish Cream

Matchstick Potatoes en Papillote, with Lemon

Raspberry and Pistachio Nut Meringue

To dress up a barbecue it is worth experimenting with different woods thrown on to the coals: fruit woods, cedar, mesquite, eucalyptus, hickory, branches of bay or other herbs. One of the most effective ruses, which cooks fish to perfection, is to steam it between long damp wild grasses. This imparts an elusive fragrance to the fish, which I can always conjure in my mind though never adequately describe. I hear sceptics muttering that presumably it tastes of grass. It is in no way reminiscent of the smell of wet grass. The flavour is very pleasant, subtle with a mysterious herbal sweetness. It is not unusual to find yourself with a surfeit of trout on your hands at some stage of the summer, so this is worthy of a try.

Really a performance for the countryside, the method calls for a large brick and iron grid assembly rather than a bijou, compact barbecue in the corner of the garden, not to mention a supply of long wild grasses, which seldom feature in urban areas.

These rustic barbecues are easily constructed. To build a good-sized circular one, first lay a circle of ten bricks. Lay a second course of bricks, offset against the first, and continue to build a well until it is ten courses high. Fill the centre with rubble and bricks, ending with a layer of bricks three bricks below the top of the well. Rest an iron grid over the centre. The barbecue now requires 'seasoning', which will take several barbecues and some rain for a good mat of ashes to form on its base.

A rustic ploy for barbecued sardines is to dig a hollow in the ground and make a fire of empty corncobs. Cover the sardines, heads, guts and all, with coarse sea salt and leave them for an hour. Boil a pan of potatoes and place the pan in the embers of the fire. Brush the salt from the sardines, gut and descale them, and skewer them on long skewers which will lie across the hollow. Now cook them over the red hot ashes. Make a sauce as follows: crush a clove of garlic with a tablespoon of parsley and a tablespoon of sweet paprika and thin the paste with 3 tablespoons of olive oil and 1 tablespoon of vinegar. Spread all sides of the grilled sardines with the mixture and eat them with the potatoes. This sauce is also delicious spread over sardines which have been dredged in seasoned flour and pan-fried.

A Spanish recipe for baked spring onions recommends that you take a dozen fat spring onions per person, place them on a bed of dried vine shoots, and set fire to these. After 20 minutes serve the onions; each person removes the charred outer layer and eats the *calcot* inside. They are eaten with the following sauce: crush a clove of garlic with a little salt and finely chopped mint in a pestle and mortar, add some roasted hazelnuts and the flesh of a grilled red pepper, crush this together into a smooth cream, then dribble in olive oil until the sauce is a dipping consistency. This performance is perhaps more easily accomplished in a food processor.

Char-grilled Fennel with Fresh Herbed Cheese

1 lb/450 g ricotta or fresh cream cheese	good Italian olive oil
2 dessertspoons finely chopped chervil, chives, parsley, fennel, lovage	lemon juice
	salt and pepper
	6 slices coarse-textured white bread
3 bulbs fennel	

Combine the cheese and herbs in a bowl, using a wooden spoon. Shape the cheese into a square or cylindrical log 7 in/18 cm long, cover it with cling-film and chill until required.

Since the fish will monopolize the barbecue, the fennel should be cooked beforehand. Char-grilled vegetables are fine served at room temperature.

Quarter the fennel bulbs by first cutting them in half vertically, slicing between the shoots, then cutting each half in half again, again vertically. Nick off any excess root, leaving enough to hold the layers together.

Steam the fennel for 5-7 minutes. Pat it dry with kitchen paper and brush it with olive oil. Season and char-grill it for 20-30 minutes until it starts to char in patches.

Char-grill the bread on a stove-top griddle.

Squeeze some lemon juice over the fennel. Serve it with slices of the herbed cheese, more olive oil trickled over and a sprinkling of salt, accompanied by the char-grilled bread.

Salmon Trout Steamed between Wild Grasses, with Samphire and Horseradish Cream

Salmon trout, large trout or small salmon are all candidates here. The salmon trout season finishes at the end of July, while salmon continues.

If rustic barbecues and wild grasses elude you, then poach the fish whole. Clean and gut the fish. Make a *court bouillon* by first bringing an equal quantity of white wine and water to boil in a large pan or fish kettle. Throw in some coarsely chopped carrot, celery, leek and onion, a *bouquet garni* of bay, parsley and thyme, some black peppercorns and a good deal of salt. If you do not possess a fish kettle with a removable grid, lay a clean tea-towel on the base of the pan and place the fish on top of it. When you come to remove the fish it can be lifted out in its sling, intact. Another tea-towel can be placed over the surface of the water to ensure that the top of the fish cooks.

Bring the *court bouillon* to the boil, immerse the fish, cover the pan tightly, turn the heat off, and leave it to poach for 2 hours as the liquid cools.

If you are barbecuing the fish, allow half an hour each side. Moisten an armful of long wild grasses and spread half of them over the barbecue grid, covering it well. Lay the fish on top and lay the remaining grass over so that it is completely nested in. The grasses will hiss as the fish is steamed. Keep the grass moist by spraying it with water when necessary.

Samphire

The season for samphire runs from Mid-summer's Day through to August, although this gets earlier each year as the demand for it and knowledge of its existence grow. I recently ate samphire in October, a misguided choice on my part. It had all the qualities of runner beans that have gone over the top and was most unpleasant to eat.

1 lb/450 g samphire	*1 oz/30 g butter, melted*

Pick over the samphire, discarding any tough, coloured or slimy stems. It keeps well for days, but is at its best fresh. Wash it in cold water. Just before serving the fish, blanch it for 1 minute. Drain it and toss with the melted butter.

Horseradish Cream

A perennial herb, horseradish is native to south-eastern Europe and came to northern Europe during medieval times. It can be found growing wild by streams or on waste ground. It spreads by underground runners, like mint, and has Triffid tendencies given a free rein in the garden. The root can be preserved in sand over the winter.

The root can differ in strength, so be discerning. The sauce should have a definite taste of horseradish, but not an overpowering kick.

A word of warning for the unfortunate given the task of grating the root. The odour given off plays havoc with your eyes, and the juice is none too kind on the skin. Use the fine grater on a food processor if possible. I once had the dubious pleasure of grating an armful of the stuff with a hand grater, and the memory lingers.

¼ pint/150 ml double cream	lemon juice
3-4 teaspoons finely grated horseradish	salt and pepper

Whip the cream into soft peaks, stopping well before it is stiff. Stir in the horseradish and season it with lemon juice, salt and pepper.

Matchstick Potatoes en Papillote, with Lemon

1½ lb/675 g potatoes	1 lemon
1½ oz/45 g butter	salt

Cut 6 rectangles of baking parchment paper 9 × 12 in/23 × 30 cm. Peel the potatoes and cut them into batons ⅛ in/0.5 cm square, 2-3 in/5-7.5 cm long. Rinse them and drain them thoroughly on kitchen paper. Divide these matchsticks between the pieces of parchment. Dot some butter on each one. Zest the lemon and place a few strands in each parcel. Squeeze over a little lemon juice and season with salt. Fold the edges of each parcel together into a neat airtight package.

Place the packages on a baking sheet and cook them for 15-20 minutes in a medium oven. The potatoes should be firm to the bite. Give each diner a package and savour the trapped steam.

Raspberry and Pistachio Nut Meringue

3 oz/85 g pistachio nuts	¾ pint/450 ml double cream
4 egg whites	1 lb/450 g raspberries or wild
pinch of cream of tartar	strawberries
pinch of salt	icing sugar
8 oz/225 g caster sugar	

Try to obtain ready shelled and skinned pistachios. Failing this, make sure they are unsalted, shell them and blanch them for 1 minute. Drain the nuts, place them in a tea-towel, and rub this to remove the skins. Pick off the remaining recalcitrant husks. Discard any yellow nuts, and dry the remainder in a low oven. Grind them in a coffee grinder.

Cut three circles of parchment paper 9 in/23 cm in diameter. Whisk the egg whites with the cream of tartar and salt until they are stiff. Whisk in the caster sugar 2 tablespoons at a time, beating for 20 seconds with each addition. Stir in the ground pistachios. Lay the three circles of paper on baking sheets and spread them with the meringue. Bake for 1½ hours in a low oven, at 125°C/225°F/Gas ½. Allow them to cool in the oven. Remove the paper.

Stiffly whip the cream. Assemble the meringue in layers with the cream and raspberries, ending with a layer of raspberries. The cake looks particularly pretty surrounded by roses, the whole thing dusted with icing sugar.

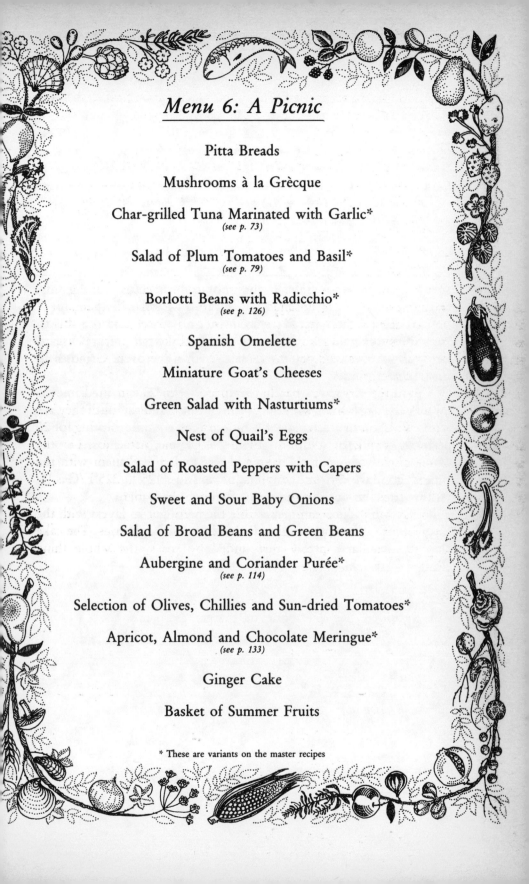

Menu 6: A Picnic

Pitta Breads

Mushrooms à la Grècque

Char-grilled Tuna Marinated with Garlic*
(see p. 73)

Salad of Plum Tomatoes and Basil*
(see p. 79)

Borlotti Beans with Radicchio*
(see p. 126)

Spanish Omelette

Miniature Goat's Cheeses

Green Salad with Nasturtiums*

Nest of Quail's Eggs

Salad of Roasted Peppers with Capers

Sweet and Sour Baby Onions

Salad of Broad Beans and Green Beans

Aubergine and Coriander Purée*
(see p. 114)

Selection of Olives, Chillies and Sun-dried Tomatoes*

Apricot, Almond and Chocolate Meringue*
(see p. 133)

Ginger Cake

Basket of Summer Fruits

* These are variants on the master recipes

In the event of a picnic one is forced to put on one's 'practical hat'. To start with, the dishes must stand up well to jostling and heat. I would opt for an array of colourful, robust little dishes spread out on a gingham cloth under a tree; some good French cider, lager and chilled Sancerre (carried to the scene wrapped in wet newspaper for quintessential picnic spirit, and to keep it cold). All this rather than tables, damask cloths, wine coolers, roulades, mousses, strawberries and cream and other such ceremony.

The only permanent fixtures in my picnic hamper are a bottle opener, a corkscrew and an 'opinel' knife, the sexy French cousin to the Swiss army knife: considerably less sophisticated, it is basically a wooden handled penknife. It may not achieve its true *métier* of prising open oysters or coarsely slicing truffles while in my hamper, but it is none the less an old friend. Most of the essentials like plates, cups and receptacles should be disposable, although cottagey china can look wonderful if you can be bothered to transport it there and home again, dirty.

A pitta bread party, or pitta bread picnic, did not strike me as a particularly attractive concept when I first came across it in an article in *Country Living* by Philippa Davenport, but it works perfectly, particularly for a large number of people. Only one word of warning – the pitta bread must be hot, otherwise some other type of good fresh bread would be better. So this is only suitable if you are travelling a short distance or have access to an oven close by.

I served the following menu on a blustery day in Hyde Park to forty people. The pitta was rushed to the picnic from my kitchen close by, insulated in foil-lined wooden crates.

Mushrooms à la Grècque

This recipe is based on one in Margaret Costa's *Four Seasons Cookery Book* — my first cookery book, well-thumbed and much loved.

³/₄ pint/450 ml water	6 parsley stalks
¹/₈ pint/75 ml olive oil	1 shallot, finely chopped
juice of ¹/₂ lemon	a good pinch of saffron
¹/₂ teaspoon salt	1 lb/450 g button mushrooms
12 black peppercorns	2 tomatoes, skinned, seeded and
¹/₄ teaspoon fennel seeds	chopped (concassée)
¹/₄ teaspoon coriander seeds	chervil leaves to garnish

Prepare an aromatic broth of all the ingredients except the mushrooms, tomatoes and chervil. Tying the seeds in a piece of muslin ensures that you do not bite on the odd remaining fennel seed or peppercorn, but it's not essential and usually I take my rustic chances. Bring the broth to the boil and simmer it for 10 minutes. Wipe the mushrooms, add them to the pan and simmer for a further 10 minutes.

Remove the mushrooms to a serving dish. Reduce the liquid to ⅛ pint/75 ml, strain it over the mushrooms, and chill them. Garnish the dish with the tomato concassée and chervil leaves.

Spanish Omelette

Apart from its role here as picnic food, Spanish omelette is one of the better Sunday night stand-bys. Visits by hordes of professional eaters over the weekend can leave the larder looking pitifully empty, but one can always hope to be left with eggs, potatoes and onions in order to fry up a Spanish omelette before expiring in front of the television. Additions of peppers, peas or tuna do not go amiss. By way of gilding the lily the omelette can be eaten with garlic cream (see recipe below) and pass as a rustic first course or lunch dish.

Just off the Portobello Road there is a café run by a Spaniard, Antonio Trillo, where my husband and his workmates often go for tortilla and coffee mid-morning. Toni has run this café for ten years, and he was brought up in Corona, Galicia, where he learnt the art of tortilla-making by watching his mother.

I tried and tried and tried to figure out a recipe for Spanish omelette which would compare to Toni's, but every time my husband's response was 'not as good as Toni's'. Standing in the face of defeat, I asked Toni if he would teach me how to produce the perfect omelette. Into the kitchen we went, where he painstakingly took me through every detail of what it is he does with four ingredients and a frying-pan that I had failed to do. Toni is so experienced in this one art that he could write a small book on the variables involved. It was a daunting process to convey to a reader something that comes across as being more instinct than method. Certainly this is not an operation that can be performed with a frying-pan in one hand and a book in the other. You need to read through the instructions, understand what you are trying to achieve, how it should all progress, then put the book down and pick the frying-pan up.

2 small onions	*olive oil*
4 medium-sized potatoes	*salt*
5 eggs	

Chop the onions. Peel and quarter the potatoes and cut them into slices ⅛ in/0.5 cm thick. These can be cooked in two ways; the important thing is to cook them together. Either deep-fry them, or heat a few tablespoons of olive oil in a frying-pan and cook them until they are soft, cooked and creamy. They should not be coloured or crisp. Cool them in a bowl, add some salt, and then break in the eggs. Combine all the ingredients with a fork.

This quantity is intended to be cooked in an 8-in/20-cm frying-pan with steep sides, giving an omelette 1 in/2.5 cm deep. It would feed 4 people as a first course, and this size is quite adequate for this picnic. If the pan is a different size, scale the ingredients down or up to accommodate it.

Over a high heat, heat a little oil in the frying-pan. When it is smoking tip out the excess. Pour in the omelette mixture, turn the heat down low, and scramble so that it thickens slightly and absorbs the oil in the pan. By turning the heat down you will cook the egg inside without burning the outer surface. Keep shaking the pan and loosening the sides of the omelette to prevent it from sticking.

The total cooking time will range between 5 and 8 minutes. Toni's recommendation was to err on the side of caution when turning the omelette over, since it can always be given a second cooking if it is underdone. So after 2-3 minutes of cooking the first side, turn it over, either by a nifty flick of the wrist like Toni, or hedge your bets and slide it on to a dinner plate and then tip it back into the pan. The underside should be mottled a light brown. If the omelette has stuck and some of its surface remains attached to the pan, loosen and discard this before returning the omelette. Re-oil the pan in the same fashion as the initial oiling until it smokes, then return the omelette. If this has happened it will require a second cooking on the first side. In this case, cook the second side over a high heat to avoid overcooking the centre, since it will now require a longer overall cooking.

While cooking the second side, periodically press the centre to test its firmness: if it is fairly hard, it has overcooked. It should be yielding and soft, indicating a runny centre. If the omelette is to be eaten cold, it should be kept on the runny side and cooked over a marginally higher heat, since the egg will continue to cook and toughen on cooling. Two minutes each side should be about right. Using a fork, tease the edges of the omelette inwards into a neat rounded edge. Depending on whether the omelette needs to be turned again, remove it to a plate.

Garlic Cream

2 heads of garlic	1 teaspoon brandy
1 tablespoon olive oil	1 teaspoon madeira
6 fl oz/175 ml double cream	salt

Place the heads of garlic, whole, into a hot oven for 20 minutes. When they are cool enough to handle, squeeze the cloves from the husk into a small saucepan. Add the olive oil, cream, brandy and madeira and cook the sauce until the cream thickens and amalgamates with the oil. Season the sauce with salt and purée it in a blender. Serve it warm over the omelette.

Miniature Goat's Cheeses

The goat's cheese needs to be the consistency of cream cheese, and lightly salted. Not the very fresh unsalted variety nor a harder, mature cheese.

4 oz/115 g goat's cheese	flaked almonds, toasted
poppy seeds	chopped hazelnuts, toasted
sesame seeds, toasted	chopped dates

Form the cheese into logs 1 in/2.5 cm long, ½ in/1.25 cm in diameter, and roll each one in a different seed or nut to provide a selection of miniature logs.

Nest of Quail's Eggs

Some florists and garden shops sell moss-lined bird's nests, which can be used to good effect to present food, particularly at cocktail parties, and are here filled with unpeeled quail's eggs. For perfectly cooked quail's eggs — a yolk cooked on the outside and moist within — lower them gently into boiling water and cook for 2½ minutes.

Salad of Roasted Peppers with Capers

This salad is a good standby for a summer starter. The peppers can be served whole rather than cut into strips.

If you are cooking the peppers under the grill or on a griddle the skin can blister and blacken without overcooking the flesh. Cooking them in a hot oven ensures a more even cooking, but care has to be taken that the flesh does not overcook. They may not appear to be cooked after 20 minutes, but after steaming them the skins should come off with ease.

4 red peppers	2 tablespoons capers
3 yellow peppers	salt and pepper
1 bunch spring onions	olive oil

Place the peppers on the grid of a grill pan in a very hot oven for 20 minutes. The skins should appear to be looser, but not too black. Put one plastic bag inside another and place the peppers inside. Seal the bag and leave them to cool. When cold enough to handle, skin and deseed them, working over the open plastic bag or a bowl so as to retain the juice. If necessary rinse them under running water and pat dry to remove remaining seeds and skin, but avoid this if possible. Slice each pepper lengthwise into thin strips. Place them in a container.

Trim the spring onions, wash them and cut them in half lengthwise. Heat a heavy cast-iron frying-pan and cover the base with a single layer of spring onions. Cook them until they are limp and speckled with black.

Mix the onions and capers with the peppers. Season, strain over the pepper juices and cover with olive oil. Leave to marinate for several hours.

Sweet and Sour Baby Onions

A relish is essential for this type of *mélange*. This recipe is taken from *A Taste of Provence* by Carey and Julian More. It accompanies a red pepper and olive salad at Café des Nattes, Avignon. Do not be alarmed by the amount of liquid at the start of the recipe – it reduces to a perfect sauce.

1 lb/450 g baby onions	*3 tablespoons tomato purée*
2 fl oz/55 ml wine vinegar	*3 oz/85 g raisins*
3 tablespoons olive oil	*bouquet garni*
2 oz/55 g sugar	*salt and pepper*

Combine all the ingredients together in a saucepan with 8 fl oz/225 ml of water. Bring to the boil and simmer uncovered for 30 minutes, until the liquid has reduced to a thick sauce. Remove the *bouquet garni* and allow the relish to cool.

Salad of Broad Beans and Green Beans

¾ lb/340 g green beans	*salt and freshly ground white*
6 oz/170 g broad beans, frozen or	*pepper*
* fresh*	*4 fl oz/115 ml arachide*
1 egg yolk	* (groundnut) oil*
¼ teaspoon grain mustard	*mint or summer savory*
squeeze of lemon juice	

Cut the tails off the green beans and cut them into 2-in/5-cm lengths. Boil them for 2-3 minutes and plunge them into cold water. Boil the broad beans for 2-3 minutes if they are frozen, longer if they are fresh. When they are cool, remove the pale husk. My husband, who gets handed this task as a form of sedentary relaxation during the evening, insists that frozen broad beans are best defrosted, skinned and then cooked. Place the beans together in a bowl.

Prepare a mayonnaise by whisking the egg yolk with the mustard, lemon juice, salt and pepper. Whisk in the oil in a thin stream until the egg yolk is saturated and too thick. Thin it with water until it is a thick pouring consistency. Finely chop a handful of mint or savory, add it to the mayonnaise, dress the salad and adjust the seasoning.

Ginger Cake

This is a good old-fashioned sticky ginger cake, and demands a day or two in an airtight container to acquire its essential characteristics.

4 oz/115 g butter	*2 eggs*
4 oz/115 g brown sugar	*8 oz/225 g plain flour*
4 oz/115 g black treacle	*½ teaspoon bicarbonate of soda*
6 oz/170 g golden syrup	*3 tablespoons whisky*
2 level teaspoons ground ginger	*2 pieces preserved ginger*
1 level teaspoon cinnamon	*4 oz/115 g sultanas*

Preheat the oven to 150°C/300°F/Gas 2. Butter and flour an 8-in/20-cm springform cake tin, lining the base.

Cream together the butter and sugar. Add the treacle, golden syrup and spices. Add the eggs and flour alternately. Warm the bicarbonate of soda with the whisky and stir it into the mixture. Chop the ginger, and stir this and the sultanas into the cake. Pour the mixture into the cake tin and bake it for 1 hour, or until a skewer comes out clean.

Remove the springform collar. When the cake is cool, store it in an airtight container for at least 24 hours before it is eaten.

Basket of Summer Fruits

There can be little more appealing than a basket on the grass filled with a medley of peaches, nectarines, apricots, cherries, figs if it is late summer, and cantaloupe or charentais melons.

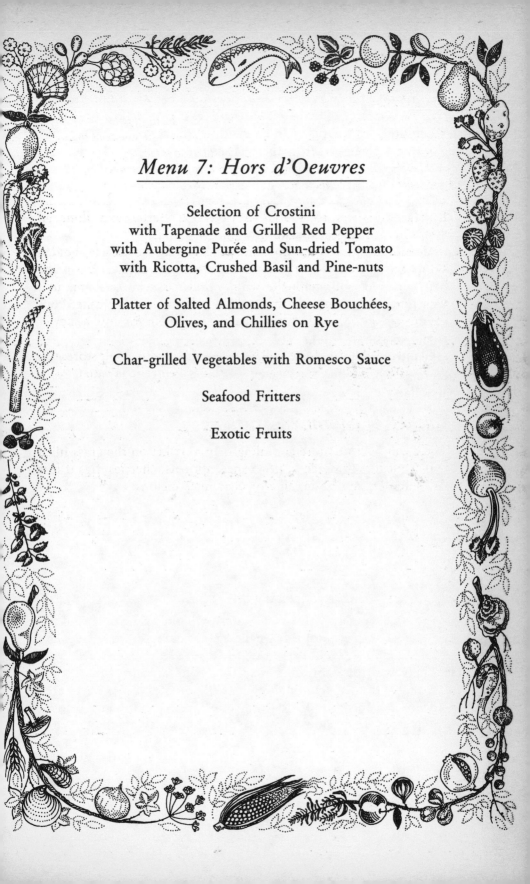

Menu 7: Hors d'Oeuvres

Selection of Crostini
with Tapenade and Grilled Red Pepper
with Aubergine Purée and Sun-dried Tomato
with Ricotta, Crushed Basil and Pine-nuts

Platter of Salted Almonds, Cheese Bouchées,
Olives, and Chillies on Rye

Char-grilled Vegetables with Romesco Sauce

Seafood Fritters

Exotic Fruits

By definition, *hors d'oeuvres* or *antipasti* are before or outside the meal. They should whet the appetite and set the juices flowing. They are additional to the menu and should be followed by a meal. It is not unusual to come across these terms used 'umbrella' fashion to encompass all cocktail party and pre-prandial snacks too. *Hors d'oeuvres* also include the delicious marinated or stuffed seafood, vegetables *à la grècque* and other little dishes that can be served on a small plate with a fork.

I delight in being the recipient of creative miniature morsels at a social function, but find it one of the least enjoyable aspects of food preparation. Catering for a party of 100 guests or more involves days on end bent double over the chopping board, eyes straining, only to emerge hideously depressed when the party's over. Life akin to an eighteenth-century lacemaker. It involves a totally different type of preparation to the relaxed, informal style of cooking which I find most pleasurable. Different types of cocktail party food suit different occasions: the subject really deserves a book. These particular 'eats' are a move away from miniature morsels which are perfect at very formal occasions. They are more substantial and best consumed with a certain inelegant gusto.

Selection of Crostini
with Tapenade and Grilled Red Pepper
with Aubergine Purée and Sun-dried Tomato
with Ricotta, Crushed Basil and Pine-nuts

TO MAKE CROÛTONS
Choose a large French stick about 2 feet/60 cm long and about 2 in/5 cm in diameter, with a thin soft crust. Thinly slice the bread to give you 50 or so croûtons. Place these on a baking sheet in the oven at 180°C/350°F/Gas 4 for 5 minutes to dry out. Paint each one sparingly with olive oil on both sides, using a pastry brush, and return them to the oven for another 10-12 minutes or until they are golden. Cool the croûtons on a sheet of greaseproof paper before storing them. They should be made on the day they are to be used.

Crostini with Tapenade and Grilled Red Pepper

(makes approx. 15)

Since tapenade keeps for several weeks in the fridge, I prefer to make double the quantity, which can also be more finely processed in a food processor than a small amount. If making a small amount, the ingredients can be reduced to a coarse purée in the food processor and then pounded to a paste in a pestle and mortar. Many people add anchovies to a tapenade; for this quantity, 2 anchovy fillets would be appropriate.

Tapenade

4 oz/115 g black olives, pitted	½ clove garlic
½ oz/15 g capers	black pepper
pinch of thyme	1 tablespoon olive oil
shot of brandy	

To assemble

1-2 red peppers	flat-leaf parsley
8 anchovies	croûtons (see above)
1 tablespoon capers	

To prepare the tapenade, finely process the olives, capers, thyme, brandy and garlic in a food processor. Add the olive oil in a slow stream, until it is the consistency of a thick spreadable paste. Season the tapenade with ground black pepper.

Heat the oven to 200°C/400°F/Gas 6 and cook the peppers for 20 minutes, using a grill pan to collect any juices that might escape – if the peppers cook in a pool of juice the flesh can char. The juices can be discarded. Place one plastic bag inside another and place the peppers inside, sealing the bag. Leave the peppers to cool and steam, which will facilitate peeling them. Remove the cores, skin and white membranes and cut the flesh into pieces 2 × 1 in (5 × 2.5 cm).

Halve the anchovies lengthwise. Pick some single leaves of flat-leaf parsley to use as a garnish.

To assemble the crostini, spread the croûtons generously with tapenade. Place a piece of pepper on top of each one, and a curled anchovy on top of this. Decorate each crostini with a caper and a leaf of parsley.

Crostini with Aubergine Purée and Sun-dried Tomato

(makes approx. 15)

Aubergine purée

2 medium-sized aubergines	juice of ½ lemon
½ clove garlic	1 tablespoon finely chopped
2 tablespoons extra virgin olive	parsley, optional
oil	salt and pepper
2 teaspoons Greek yoghurt	

To assemble

4 halves sun-dried tomato	croûtons (see above)
fresh coriander	

To prepare the aubergine purée, first place the aubergines in a hot oven at 200°C/400°F/Gas 6 for 25-30 minutes until the skins are wrinkled and charred. Roast them on a grill pan to collect any juices that may be exuded. (If the aubergines cook sitting in a pool of their own juices, they can burn and this can flavour the flesh.)

Remove the skin from the aubergines, place the flesh in a sieve and press out all the juices. Purée the flesh and the garlic in a food processor. Add the olive oil in a thin stream. If large aubergines have been used, pass the purée through a sieve to remove any seeds. Mix in the yoghurt, lemon juice and parsley. The size of aubergines varies, so be guided by taste and consistency rather than amounts. Season the purée well; it requires a fairly hefty dose of salt.

Cut the sun-dried tomato into strips. Pick single leaves of coriander.

To assemble the crostini, spread the croûtons with generous mounds of aubergine purée, lay a strip of sun-dried tomato on each one, and garnish with a coriander leaf.

Crostini with Ricotta, Crushed Basil and Pine-nuts

(makes approx. 15)

Try to buy ricotta cut from a whole cheese and not packaged in a plastic carton: ask to taste it first to assure yourself it is fresh.

5 oz/140 g ricotta	1 tablespoon pine-nuts
basil	croûtons (see above)
1 tablespoon extra virgin olive oil	

Thinly slice the ricotta into blocks 2 × 1 in/5 × 2.5 cm. Make a chiffonade of basil by placing several medium-sized leaves one on top of the other, rolling the leaves up tightly lengthwise, and finely slicing across the roll, to give thin strips. Place a small handful of the chiffonade in a pestle and mortar and cover it with the olive oil. Crush it gently to release some of the essence from the leaves. Add the pine-nuts.

To assemble the crostini, place a slice of ricotta on each croûton, and put a small teaspoonful of the basil and pine-nuts on top of this.

Platter of Salted Almonds, Cheese Bouchées, Olives, and Chillies on Rye

Salted Almonds

In *Spices, Salt and Aromatics in the English Kitchen*, Elizabeth David details how perfect salted almonds can be produced, a method devised by her Sudanese cook, Suliman.

Gather together 1 teaspoon of almond oil or butter, ½ lb/225 g of whole blanched almonds, 3 tablespoons of fine crystal sea salt and some cayenne pepper. Rub a baking tin with the oil and lay the almonds in it. Place the tray in a low oven for 45 minutes until the almonds are a pale golden colour. Lay a sheet of baking parchment on the kitchen work surface with the salt scattered over it. Place the almonds on this and rub the crystals around the almonds so that some of the salt adheres to them. Gather up the sides of the paper, twisting them together into a purse. Put this aside for 5-6 hours. Open up the parcel, shake the almonds free from excess salt and sprinkle a hint of cayenne pepper over them − this piquancy is all-important. The almonds can now be devoured, as soon as possible, for within 24 hours they will lose their squeaky-to-the-bite freshness.

Under duress I have deviated from this carefully devised ritual and roasted the almonds in a very hot oven for 10 minutes, leaving them to salt for only 1 hour. They may lose a couple of points, but they still get high marks.

Cheese Bouchées

These are light crisp cheese savouries which are golden and puffed when cooked. They can be sprinkled with caraway, cumin, celery, sesame or poppy seeds, a personal preference being cumin seeds. They are best eaten within 24 hours.

6 oz/170 g plain flour	6 oz/170 g mature Cheddar,
¾ teaspoon salt	grated
3 oz/85 g butter	2 eggs
¾ teaspoon mustard	caraway, cumin, celery, sesame,
1 oz/30 g freshly grated	or poppy seeds
Parmesan	

Place the flour and salt in a food processor, add the butter and process the mixture to crumbs. Mix in the mustard, Parmesan and Cheddar. Bring the dough together with one of the eggs. Wrap it in cling-film and rest it for 15 minutes in the fridge.

Preheat the oven to 200°C/400°F/Gas 6. Thinly roll the dough ⅛ in/0.5 cm thick. Cut it into circles using a biscuit cutter, or into triangles or squares. Place the bouchées on a baking sheet, beat the remaining egg and lightly glaze the biscuits. Scatter seeds of your choice over them and bake for 8-14 minutes. Keep a careful eye on the bouchées, removing them as they become puffed and golden. Cool them on a rack.

Olives

Olives straight from the tree are bitter and not suitable for eating, so they must be cured. Different varieties of olives suit different preparations. My favourites are the black olives cured in a Provençal fashion, dried and marinated with oil and herbs. Also good are the green olives which have been cracked and cured in brine with garlic and spices, and the Greek Kalamata olives. The Kalamata olive is specifically an eating olive, though it is also good for producing olive oil, as its oiliness suggests. Try to obtain a selection of different kinds.

Chillies on Rye

My local Spanish delicatessen sells pickled chillies in a barrel alongside different varieties of olives. Long, pale green, piquantly hot and salty, they marry perfectly with Mexican food, particularly avocados and tomatoes, but a personal passion is to pair them with chilled Greek yoghurt or *fromage frais*.

---

8 preserved chillies   *2 tablespoons Greek yoghurt*
2 slices wholegrain rye bread or
   pumpernickel

Rinse and dry the chillies. Remove the core and squeeze out the main clutch of seeds at the head, then slice them thickly.

Cut the rye bread into quarters, removing any crusts. Put a dollop of Greek yoghurt on each one and adorn with sliced chilli.

Char-grilled Vegetables with Romesco Sauce

Cut aubergines, courgettes, some red or yellow peppers and mushrooms into ¼-½-in/0.75-1.25-cm dice. Thread a cube of each vegetable on to a cocktail stick, so that the tip of the stick is encased by the last morsel. Repeat until you have used up all the vegetables.

Paint them with olive oil and lightly season with salt and pepper. Char-grill them on both sides or under a conventional grill. They are still good having cooled a little. Serve them with a bowl of Romesco sauce.

Romesco Sauce

Fill an azure blue china bowl with this sauce, a Mediterranean burnt orange, and eat it with a plate of char-grilled vegetables, crisply pan-fried sardines, or simply with raw vegetables. Its wholesome earthy texture comes from the tomatoes, which go in unpeeled and unseeded, and the ground nuts. It achieves a wonderful blend of spices and flavours without being rich. Of the many variations of Romesco sauce to be had, these quantities and ingredients are a good balance of the different flavours involved.

1 red pepper	*knife tip of crushed dried chilli*
3 fl oz/85 ml olive oil plus some	*knife tip of paprika*
for frying	*8 oz/225 g tomatoes, quartered*
1 oz/30 g day-old white bread	*1 scant tablespoon sherry vinegar*
2½ oz/70 g blanched almonds	*salt and pepper*
1 clove garlic	

Roast the red pepper in a hot oven for 20 minutes according to the instructions on p. 108. Skin and dessed it.

Heat a little olive oil in a frying-pan and fry the bread on both sides to a deep golden colour.

Toast the almonds in the oven for 7-8 minutes at 180°C/350°F/ Gas 4, then grind them finely in an electric coffee grinder. Place the garlic and fried bread in the bowl of a food processor and process them as finely as possible. Add the ground almonds, chilli, paprika, tomatoes and red pepper and reduce them to a paste. Trickle in the olive oil with the motor running, then add the vinegar. Check the seasoning.

Seafood Fritters

A selection of these fritters would produce a good *fritto misto di mare* as part of a meal. The mussel batter could also be used as a general batter to coat other fish.

Mussel Fritters

The art of dropping the batter into the hot oil will take a few tries – but part of the charm of these fritters lies in their rough, misshapen character. They must be eaten hot from the pan, crisp and puffed up – after 10 minutes they start to deflate, becoming greasy and soft.

Autumn is the season for English mussels, but some fishmongers will sell imported ones all the year round.

1 lb/450 g mussels	*2 tablespoons olive oil*
mussel liquor, made up to 7 fl	*1 egg, separated*
oz/200 ml with water	*pure olive oil for deep-frying*
3½ oz/100 g plain white flour	*finely chopped flat-leaf parsley*

Clean and steam open the mussels according to the instructions on p. 55. Remove them from their shells and chop the flesh finely.

Strain the liquor through a sieve lined with kitchen paper or muslin, and make it up to 7 fl oz/200 ml with water.

Add the flour, olive oil and egg yolk to the liquid, beating it into a smooth batter. Add the mussel flesh. Stiffly beat the egg white and stir it into the batter.

Heat plenty of oil in a saucepan. Drop the batter in small spoonfuls into the hot oil, turning the fritters over as the underside browns. Drain them on absorbent paper and sprinkle them with finely chopped parsley.

Salt Cod Fritters with Skordalia

½ lb/225 g salt cod	*1 heaped tablespoon coriander,*
bouquet garni of bay leaf, sprig	*finely chopped*
of thyme and parsley	*2 small egg yolks*
1 lb/450 g potatoes	*breadcrumbs*
	pure olive oil for deep-frying

Rinse the salt cod to remove as much surface salt as possible. Place it skin side up in a bowl, cover it with water and soak it for 24 hours, changing the water several times. Sometimes the cod can still be excessively salty even after soaking it in this fashion. If possible leave it overnight in a bowl in a sink with water constantly running into the bowl, taking care that there is no conceivable way the plug can become blocked.

Place the cod in a saucepan, cover it with water, and add the *bouquet garni*. Bring the water to the boil and simmer for 10 minutes. Remove the fish, and when it is cool enough to handle remove the skin and bones and mash the flesh into fine flakes.

Peel the potatoes and boil them for 30 minutes. Drain them in a sieve and allow any surface moisture to evaporate. Pass them through a mouli-légumes or a sieve. Mix them with the flaked salt cod. Add the chopped coriander and bind the mixture with the egg yolks.

Make fritters the size of a large cherry, using the palms of your hands, and roll them in breadcrumbs. It should not be necessary to roll them in beaten egg first. Larger fishcakes could also be made as part of a main meal.

Heat plenty of oil in a saucepan, and when it is hot deep-fry the fishcakes to a deep gold. Serve them with the skordalia.

Skordalia

3 slices white bread	1 dessertspoon vinegar
2-3 cloves garlic	5 tablespoons olive oil
salt	1 oz/30 g ground almonds

Cut the crusts off the bread. Soak the bread in water, then squeeze out most of the liquid but not all of it. Place in a food processor. Crush the garlic to a paste with a little salt. Add the garlic and vinegar to the food processor, and reduce the ingredients to a thick cream. With the motor running, add the olive oil in a thin stream, then add the ground almonds.

Squid Rings

1 lb/450 g small squid	pure olive oil for deep-frying
flour	basil or parsley, finely chopped
salt and pepper	

Clean and prepare the squid according to the instructions on p. 55. Cut them into thin rings. Season the flour with salt and pepper.

Heat plenty of oil in a saucepan. Dredge the squid rings in the seasoned flour and throw them, large handfuls at a time, into the hot oil. Remove them after 20-30 seconds. If the oil is hot enough they will be golden.

Drain them briefly on absorbent paper and sprinkle them with chopped basil or parsley.

Exotic Fruits

A plate of chilled ripe fruits served with champagne at a cocktail party or during the late morning is perfect for hot weather and as a palate cleanser. It has the same appeal as *crudités* for those who do not wish to indulge in richer offerings. Cut the fruit as befits, and put some cocktail sticks on the plate. Make up skewers of different berries using raspberries, blueberries, loganberries, blackberries, redcurrants and blackcurrants. Cube an orange-fleshed charentais or canteloupe melon, and arrange a pile of strawberries, hulls intact, or quarter some figs. Select some apricots, peaches, nectarines, papaya or grapes. Toss some cherries into a bowl of crushed ice or strew around some Cape gooseberries, petals open.

Autumn

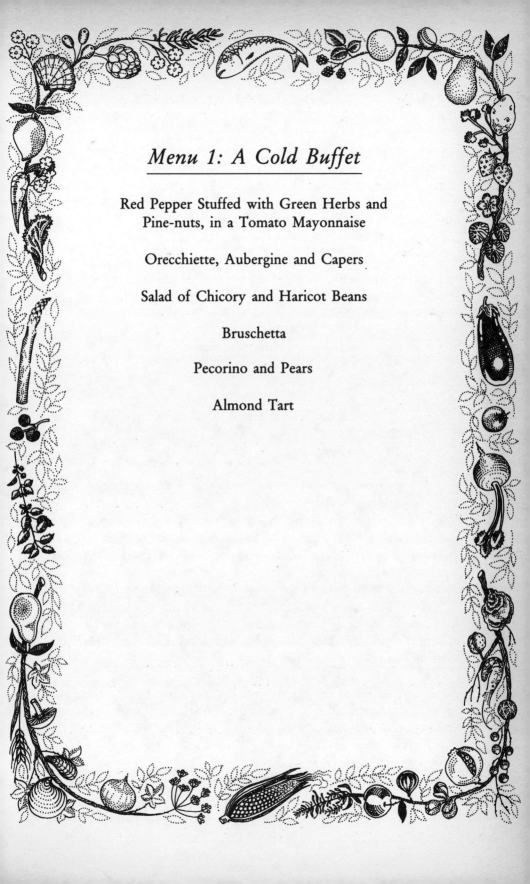

Menu 1: A Cold Buffet

Red Pepper Stuffed with Green Herbs and
Pine-nuts, in a Tomato Mayonnaise

Orecchiette, Aubergine and Capers

Salad of Chicory and Haricot Beans

Bruschetta

Pecorino and Pears

Almond Tart

Red Pepper Stuffed with Green Herbs and Pine-nuts, in a Tomato Mayonnaise

Prepared, shop-bought tomato sauce can be used in this recipe. To prepare it at home, however, sweat a couple of shallots in butter for a few minutes, then add 3 lb/1.4 kg of sliced tomatoes, cover the pan and cook over a very low heat for 30-40 minutes. Liquidize the mixture, pass through a sieve, and season the sauce.
Brioche makes wonderful breadcrumbs.

6 medium-sized red peppers	*2 tablespoons fennel seeds*
10 oz/285 g parsley	*6 oz/170 g crabmeat (optional)*
1½ oz/45 g butter	*salt and pepper*
2 anchovies (optional)	*2 eggs, beaten*
10 oz/285 g cooked spinach,	*fresh breadcrumbs*
* chopped*	*20 fl oz/565 g prepared tomato*
2 oz/55 g pine-nuts	* sauce*

Mayonnaise

3 egg yolks	*salt*
½ teaspoon Dijon mustard	*15 fl oz/425 ml olive oil*

Cut the top from each pepper and reserve it. Remove the seeds and white membranes where possible.

Pull the parsley from the stalk, wash and coarsely chop it. Melt the butter in a frying-pan, add the anchovies (if using) and crush them to a paste. Add the parsley and cook it for a few minutes, then add the spinach and cook gently for 5 minutes.

Toast the pine-nuts in the oven to a golden brown. Crush the fennel seeds in a pestle and mortar to break them up a little. Add the nuts, seeds and crabmeat (if using) to the spinach and parsley and season the stuffing. Mix in the eggs and add breadcrumbs until the stuffing is firm.

Stuff each pepper with the filling so that it comes to within ½ in/1.25 cm of the top of the pepper. Replace the lid of each one and lay them on their sides in a casserole. Pour over the tomato sauce and cover the casserole.

Heat the oven to 150°C/300°F/Gas 2. Bake the peppers for 1 hour, turning them after ½ hour.

Allow the peppers to cool. Remove them from the sauce and peel off the skin where possible — it is not essential to remove every last trace.

Make a mayonnaise: beat the egg yolks with the mustard and a pinch of salt. Whisk in the oil in a thin stream until the egg yolks are saturated and the sauce is too thick. Add about two-thirds of the tomato sauce to the mayonnaise, continuing to add it as flavour and consistency dictate. The desired result is a rich pouring sauce which tastes distinctly of tomatoes, rather than a flavoured mayonnaise. Season the sauce.

Cut the peppers into ½-in/1.25-cm slices and either place them on a pool of the sauce or pour the sauce over.

Orecchiette, Aubergine and Capers

Orecchiette, or little ears, are small, thick, shell-shaped pasta with an unusual and pleasant firmness. Traditional to Apulia, they are made without eggs, from durum wheat semolina and water. Time-consuming to make and shape by hand, it is best to buy them from an Italian delicatessen.

1 large aubergine	3 fl oz/85 ml olive oil and extra
salt and pepper	for frying
6 sprigs oregano	9 oz/255 g orecchiette
	1 oz/30 g capers

Cut the aubergine into ½-in/1.25-cm slices. Salt them on both sides and leave them in a colander for ½ hour to exude their bitter juices; this also decreases their absorbency when they come to be fried. Rinse and dry them.

Coarsely chop the oregano leaves and place them in a pestle and mortar with a little of the olive oil. Crush the leaves to release their essence and add the remaining oil. Bring a large pan of water to the boil and cook the pasta, leaving it firm to the bite. Dress it while hot with the oil and herbs and season it.

Heat 2 tablespoons of olive oil in a frying-pan and cook the aubergine slices in batches until they are a deep brown on both sides. Cut them into strips or cubes. Coarsely chop the capers. Toss together the pasta, capers and aubergine.

Salad of Chicory and Haricot Beans

The principle of this salad is to offset the sweet and dry texture of the beans with the crisp, bitter, succulent leaves. It can be extended to other types of bean and leaves with similar qualities. The picnic menu (p. 103) suggests a salad of borlotti beans and radicchio, which would give a pretty combination of the pink beans with the crimson-streaked radicchio.

This method of cooking beans renders perfectly cooked beans, skins intact.

---

6 oz/170 g haricot beans　　　　*3 tablespoons finely chopped*
2 cloves garlic, crushed　　　　　　*parsley*
3 small heads chicory　　　　　　*juice of ½ lemon*
3 fl oz/85 ml olive oil　　　　　　*salt*

Place the beans in a large bowl, fill the bowl with water and leave to soak overnight.

Preheat the oven to 170°C/325°F/Gas 3. Rinse and drain the beans, put them in a flameproof casserole and cover them with water by 2 in/5 cm. No salt should be added until the beans are cooked, otherwise it will toughen the skins. Bring the beans to the boil on top of the stove, skim any surface foam and add the crushed garlic. Cover the casserole and place it in the centre of the oven for 50 minutes to 1 hour. Drain the beans into a bowl and allow them to cool.

Slice the chicory and mix it with the beans. Add the olive oil and the parsley, followed by the lemon juice to taste. Season the salad with salt.

Bruschetta

I have a whimsical longing for the bruschetta bar to replace the English sandwich bar. Bruschetta is peasant-style garlic bread: thick slices of coarse-textured white bread, char-grilled, rubbed with garlic, an excellent olive oil liberally trickled over. It can then be embellished at your fancy with any arrangement of ripe tomatoes, olives, anchovies, capers, rocquette, thinly sliced pecorino or Parmesan, grilled peppers, mushrooms, courgettes, tapenade or any number of other foods.

6 slices coarse-textured white bread, a day old	1 clove garlic best Italian extra virgin olive oil

Heat the char-grill and toast the bread on both sides. Give one side of the toast a cursory rub with the garlic and lightly soak it with olive oil.

Pecorino and Pears

Pecorino and pears marry in their native fashion in the way that apples and Cheddar do. Select pears in their fleeting moment of perfection: peel, quarter and core them and serve them with thinly shaved pecorino.

Almond Tart

Almond tart is a contemporary classic on restaurant menus, but I am unsure who the original mastermind behind this particular version would be. It is equally good with some fruit mixed into the almond cream: apricots, cranberries and cherries spring to mind.

I normally make it in a 12-in/30-cm tart case, using double the quantities given here, which feeds 10-12 people. Serve it with whipped cream, *crème fraîche* or a rich and tart fruit dish.

Pastry

6 oz/170 g plain flour 2 oz/55 g caster sugar 3 oz/85 g butter	1 egg yolk orange juice

Filling

4 oz/115 g unsalted butter 4 oz/115 g caster sugar 2 eggs (size 5)	4 oz/115 g ground almonds 1 tablespoon kirsch 3 tablespoons flaked almonds

To make the pastry, first place the flour, sugar and butter together in the bowl of a food processor and process them to crumbs. Add the egg yolk and enough orange juice to bring the dough together.

Butter and flour a shallow-sided 9-in/23-cm tart tin and press the dough into it. Chill this for 1 hour. Should you be fortunate enough to possess a large freezer, tart cases can be frozen at this stage and baked from frozen when required. It is very useful to be able to dig out a sweet or savoury pastry case at whim.

Line the pastry case with foil and baking beans and bake it for 10 minutes at 180°C/350°F/Gas 4 until it has set and just started to colour – it will receive a second baking, so it should not be completely cooked at this stage. Remove the foil and beans and turn the oven down to 170°C/325°F/Gas 3.

Cream together the butter and sugar for the filling. Separate the eggs. Add the egg yolks and ground almonds to the butter and sugar, and stir in the kirsch. Whisk the egg white and lightly fold it into the mixture. Spread the mixture over the base of the pastry case and scatter the flaked almonds over. (If you are including fruit, mix half of it into the almond cream, spread this into the pastry case and scatter the remaining fruit and flaked almonds over.) Bake the tart for 30-40 minutes. When it is cool, dust it with icing sugar.

Menu 2: A Cold Buffet

Tartlets with Grilled Courgettes
and Parsley Purée

Seafood Salad with Saffron Cream

Wild Rice and Fennel Salad

Ginger, Almond and Fig Meringue

Tartlets with Grilled Courgettes and Parsley Purée

This parsley purée is a wonderful vivid green, and the tartlets look particularly attractive with the red sun-dried tomatoes dotted over them. The purée tastes more of an intensely flavoured spinach than of parsley; it is also good thinned with vegetable stock to make a soup. The purée does deteriorate quite rapidly, so prepare it as close to the time of serving as possible.

Tartlets

3 sheets filo pastry (approx.)	*1 oz/30 g unsalted butter, melted*

Parsley purée

14 oz/400 g parsley (curly or flat) *3 tablespoons* crème fraîche	*salt and pepper* *vinegar*

To assemble

8 oz/225 g courgettes *olive oil*	*6 halves sun-dried tomato* *salt and pepper*

Preheat the oven to 170°C/325°F/Gas 3. Prepare the tartlet cases first. Paint a sheet of filo pastry with melted butter, keeping the remaining sheets covered to avoid them drying out. Cut into six squares and line two 4-in/10-cm tartlet cases with three squares each, so that the corners form petals. Repeat this process with the remaining sheets of filo. Bake the tartlets for 8-10 minutes or until they are golden.

Strip the parsley leaves off the stalk. Bring a large pan of water to the boil and cook the parsley for 10 minutes. Strain, pressing out most of the water, then place it in a food processor with the *crème fraîche* and reduce it to a purée. Season with salt, pepper and vinegar.

Cut the courgettes on the bias into thin strips ⅛ in/0.5 cm thick (a mandolin would be useful here). Paint them on either side with olive oil and season them. Char-grill them on both sides and place them in a bowl with some olive oil poured over. Cut the sun-dried tomatoes into strips.

To assemble the tartlets, spread some of the parsley purée on the base of each case, with some of the courgette ribbons folded on top. Place some sun-dried tomato strips here and there.

Seafood Salad with Saffron Cream

Mussels, prawns and squid are available from most fishmongers at this time of year, but you can use any other shellfish which entice you: the mussel liquor can be substituted with a reduced fish stock. Not everyone likes squid, and scallops are a safer choice if you are worried about this.

The seafood and saffron cream can also be used as a hot sauce for pasta, or warm over dressed spinach leaves.

3 lb/1.4 kg fresh mussels	4 oz/115 g button mushrooms
4 fl oz/115 ml white wine	salad leaves – ideally baby
3 small squid	spinach, otherwise oakleaf, red
4 oz/115 g dwarf beans, sugar	and green batavia, mâche, cos
snaps or mangetout	3 tomatoes, peeled and seeded
8 oz/225 g fresh shelled prawns	

Saffron cream

9 fl oz/250 ml double cream	mussel liquor
1 sachet powdered saffron	freshly ground white pepper
(1/8 teaspoon)	

Vinaigrette

1 dessertspoon sherry vinegar	1/4 teaspoon mustard
1/4 teaspoon salt	4 tablespoons olive oil

Soak the mussels in cold water for 30 minutes. Discard any that do not close when sharply tapped, or any with broken shells. Remove the beards and scrub them.

Heat the wine in a large saucepan, add the mussels, cover the pan with a tightly fitting lid and steam them open for about 5 minutes, shaking the pan from time to time. Leave the mussels to cool in the pan for a short while. Remove them from their shells into a bowl and cover them with a small amount of mussel liquor. Strain the remaining liquor through muslin or a sieve lined with kitchen paper into a small saucepan.

Prepare the squid by pulling the head away from the bag. Pull out the pen and squeeze out any other substances from the sac. Remove the thin porphyry-coloured membrane and rinse the sac inside and out under running water. Slice into rings. Cut the tentacles from the head and divide them.

Bring the mussel liquor to the boil. Add the squid, cook it for 30 seconds, then remove it to the bowl containing the mussels. Reduce the remaining liquor until only 3 or 4 tablespoons remain, and reserve it in a cup. Make the saffron cream by heating the cream with the saffron until it starts to thicken. Add the mussel liquor to taste. It is unlikely to require any further salt, but season it with pepper.

If you are using dwarf beans, halve them and boil them for a couple of minutes, leaving them firm to the bite. If you are using mangetout or sugar snaps, blanch them for 30 seconds.

Mix together the mussels, squid and shelled prawns with the saffron cream. Slice the mushrooms and add them to the seafood.

Make a vinaigrette by whisking together the vinegar, salt and mustard until the salt dissolves, then add the olive oil.

To assemble the salad, toss the salad greens and the cooked beans with the vinaigrette and scatter them on a large serving plate. Quarter the tomatoes and tuck them between the salad leaves. Place the seafood over the leaves.

Wild Rice and Fennel Salad

3 oz/85 g wild rice	*2 tablespoons finely chopped*
3 oz/85 g long grain white rice	*parsley*
1 small bulb fennel	*sprigs of feathery fennel to*
1 teaspoon fennel seeds	*garnish (optional)*
zest of 1 orange, finely chopped	

Vinaigrette

1 dessertspoon sherry vinegar	*¼ teaspoon mustard*
¼ teaspoon salt	*8 dessertspoons olive oil*

Boil the wild rice in salted water for 40 minutes. Strain it into a sieve and run cold water through it. Prepare the white rice in the same way, cooking it for 15 minutes.

Cut the fennel into ¼-in/0.75-cm dice and blanch them for 1 minute. Coarsely crush the fennel seeds in a pestle and mortar.

Prepare a vinaigrette by whisking the vinegar with the salt and mustard until the salt dissolves, then add the oil.

Place all the salad ingredients together in a bowl and dress them shortly before serving. The salad can be garnished with sprigs of feathery fennel.

Ginger, Almond and Fig Meringue

This dessert is very simple to make, and other dried fruits, nuts or chocolate can be used instead of those listed. Like all meringues it is rich and fairly sweet, though it can be toned down by serving it with fruit. A more wicked indulgence would be to smother it with whipped cream and uncork the Armagnac.

Best eaten the day it is made, it will hold till the following day, but not much beyond that.

4 oz/115 g whole almonds,	*4 egg whites*
blanched	*8 oz/225 g caster sugar*
5 oz/140 g dried figs	*½ pint/300 ml double cream*
3 oz/85 g preserved ginger	

Preheat the oven to 170°C/325°F/Gas 3. Coarsely chop the almonds and toast them in the oven for 10 minutes. Chop the figs and ginger.

Stiffly beat the egg whites, gradually adding the sugar, 2 tablespoons at a time, beating for 20 seconds between each addition. The resulting meringue should be stiff and glossy.

Fold the dry ingredients into the meringue, and spoon the mixture into an 8-in/20-cm cake tin with a removable collar. Bake the cake for 35 minutes or until a skewer comes out clean from the centre. Run a knife around the collar, and cool the cake.

Whip the cream and spread it over the meringue. Chill it until you are ready to serve it.

Menu 3: A Hot Buffet

A Catalan Casserole with Pear and
Caramelized Onions

Spinach with Pine-nuts

Stoved Potatoes with Rosemary

Selection of Spanish Cheeses

Chocolate Fondant Cake

A Catalan Casserole with Pear and Caramelized Onions

Paprika, a spice normally associated with Hungarian cooking, is also widely used in Spanish dishes, where it is known as *pimentón*. Paprika is the ground seeds of the sweet red pepper, the pimento. Its gourmet value is graded according to its hue, ranging from rust to scarlet and from faintly hot to sweet. The shelf-life of a tin once open is short, and paprika past its best will ruin a dish. If you rarely use it, it is worth buying it fresh each time in a small quantity. The amount used in this recipe can range from a teaspoon to a tablespoon, depending on its heat. Ideally, use sweet and essentially mild paprika, to a generous tune. The Spanish delicatessen where I buy paprika stocks both sweet and hot varieties, and each tin is marked accordingly, but I doubt if this is the case with supermarket brands.

A *picada* is a ground preparation usually containing garlic, nuts, fried bread and spices. Added to a dish while it is cooking, it thickens and flavours it. It is a useful ploy to enrich otherwise thin and unexciting vegetarian stews or soups.

Onions

2 tablespoons olive oil	2 level teaspoons sugar
2 Spanish onions	

Picada

olive oil	4 tomatoes, skinned, seeded and
1 slice day-old white bread	diced
1 clove garlic	1 tablespoon paprika (see above)
1½ oz/45 g almonds, toasted	1 sachet saffron
1 medium onion	(⅛ teaspoon)

Casserole

8 oz/225 g carrots	8 oz/225 g chickpeas, cooked
2 unripe pears	7 oz/200 g cannellini or haricot
8 oz/225 g butternut squash	beans, cooked
8 oz/225 g green beans	salt and pepper

To prepare the caramelized onions, heat 2 tablespoons of olive oil in a frying-pan, slice the Spanish onions and cook them for 10 minutes. Add the sugar and cook them for another 15-17 minutes until they are nicely golden and almost burnt in places.

Prepare the *picada* by first heating 2 tablespoons of olive oil in a frying-pan and frying the bread to a deep golden. Allow it to cool. Finely chop the garlic and sauté it momentarily. Reduce the bread and garlic to a paste in a food processor. Grind the almonds in an electric grinder and combine them with the bread and garlic paste.

Finely chop the onion and sauté it in a tablespoon of oil for 3 minutes. Add the tomatoes and paprika and cook over a low heat for 5 minutes. Combine the two mixtures and blend in the saffron.

Bring 2 pints/1.1 litres of water to the boil in a large pan and salt it well. Peel and slice the carrots and peel, core and cube the pears. Cube the squash and cut the beans into 1-in/2.5-cm lengths.

Add the pear and carrots to the water and cook for 5 minutes. Add the squash, green beans, chickpeas, cannellini or haricot beans, and cook the casserole for a further 5 minutes. Stir in the *picada* and cook the casserole for another few minutes. Adjust the seasoning.

Serve the casserole in soup bowls, with the caramelized onions scattered over.

Spinach with Pine-nuts

Spinach with pine-nuts and raisins is a classic Catalan dish. Sadly, however, the addition of raisins here would make the menu too sweet as a whole. If you want to make the dish on another occasion, fry 1½ oz/45 g of raisins with the pine-nuts until they plump up into golden cushions, and stir them into the spinach. If preferred, the spinach can be cooked in a tightly covered pan, with only the water which clings to the leaves. Cook it for 5-7 minutes until it collapses, then press out the water in a sieve and coarsely chop it, add some butter and olive oil and season it. Use 3 lb/1.4 kg of spinach if you are cooking it this way.

2 lb/0.9 kg spinach	*salt and pepper*
butter	*2 oz/55 g pine-nuts*
olive oil	

Wash and pick over the spinach. Dry it thoroughly and tear it into large strips if the leaves are large. Heat a small knob of butter and a tablespoon of olive oil in a frying-pan or large saucepan, throw in some of the spinach and toss it until it is coated with the oil and beginning to wilt. Cover the pan and cook it for 1 minute. Remove the spinach to a bowl and season it. Cook the remaining spinach in the same way. Fry the pine-nuts, also in butter and olive oil, and stir them into the spinach.

Stoved Potatoes with Rosemary

2½ lb/1.1 kg potatoes	*4 cloves garlic*
olive oil	*5 sprigs rosemary*
salt and pepper	

Peel the potatoes, halve or quarter them, and slice them thickly. Coat them with olive oil and season them with salt and pepper. Place them in a heavy-bottomed saucepan with 2 tablespoons of water. Peel and halve the garlic cloves, and tuck them and the rosemary between the potatoes. Cover the pan tightly and cook the potatoes over the very lowest heat for 25-30 minutes, stirring them after 15 minutes. They should not brown.

Serve the potatoes as a side dish to the casserole, with the greens.

Selection of Spanish Cheeses

Spain not being traditionally renowned for its cheeses, it is refreshing to find a number of high-quality Spanish cheeses in an increasing number of outlets. Mainly local farmhouse cheeses, they rely on the whole on sheep's and goat's milk which is sometimes blended with cow's milk. Often the milk of a specific breed of sheep or goat is used to make a particular cheese. Some cheeses are distinguished by the Denominación de Origen. A cheese to look out for is Guzmán, a cheese preserved in olive oil in a tin, where it matures for up to two years. Flavoursome and hard, it is hand-made with the milk from a flock of Churra sheep. Pico-Cabrales is a semi-soft blue cheese made from cow's milk. Comparable to Roquefort, it is wrapped in maple leaves and matured in a similar fashion in natural caves, where the air currents are essential to the process. Manchego is perhaps the best known of Spanish cheeses.

Protected by the D/O designation, it is a sheep's milk cheese, aged for varying lengths of time, and comes as a round weighing 5½-6½ lb/2.5-3 kilos. Menorca is the home of Mahón, a strongly-flavoured cow's milk cheese whose rind is brushed with olive oil and paprika during the maturation process. It can be eaten spread with olive oil and scattered with a few leaves of tarragon.

Chocolate Fondant Cake

This cake is rich, with a heavy, truffle-like texture. Unrelentingly chocolate, it should satiate even those for whom chocolate is an obsession.

Cake

8 oz/225 g bitter chocolate	6 oz/170 g caster sugar plus 1
6 oz/170 g unsalted butter	tablespoon
4 tablespoons strong black coffee	2 oz/55 g plain flour
4 eggs	1 heaped teaspoon baking
	powder

Chocolate glaze

8 oz/225 g bitter chocolate	2 tablespoons coffee or brandy
2 oz/55 g unsalted butter	

Melt the chocolate and butter together. Stir in the coffee. Separate the eggs. Whisk the egg yolks and the 6 oz/170 g of sugar together until they are pale and thick; add the chocolate. Mix in the flour and baking powder.

Whisk the egg whites until they are stiff, add the remaining tablespoon of sugar, and continue whisking for 20 seconds. Incorporate the egg whites into the cake mixture as deftly as possible. If you are using a food processor, a quick burst at high speed will do it.

Line an 8-in/20-cm springform cake tin with baking parchment and butter it. Pour the cake mixture into the tin and give it several sharp taps on the work surface to eliminate any air pockets. Cook the cake for 55 minutes at 170°C/325°F/Gas 3. Loosen the springform collar and allow the cake to cool. If the cake is to be iced, slice off the pale, hard crust on the surface; for a totally flat surface it can be inverted and the underside iced.

To make the glaze, melt half the chocolate and butter over a low heat and add 1 tablespoon of coffee or brandy. Spread over the cake and around the sides, using a palette knife. Allow to set. Repeat the process with the remaining ingredients.

The cake can be decorated with chocolate leaves or curls. For a birthday, pipe it with white icing and surround it with white flowers.

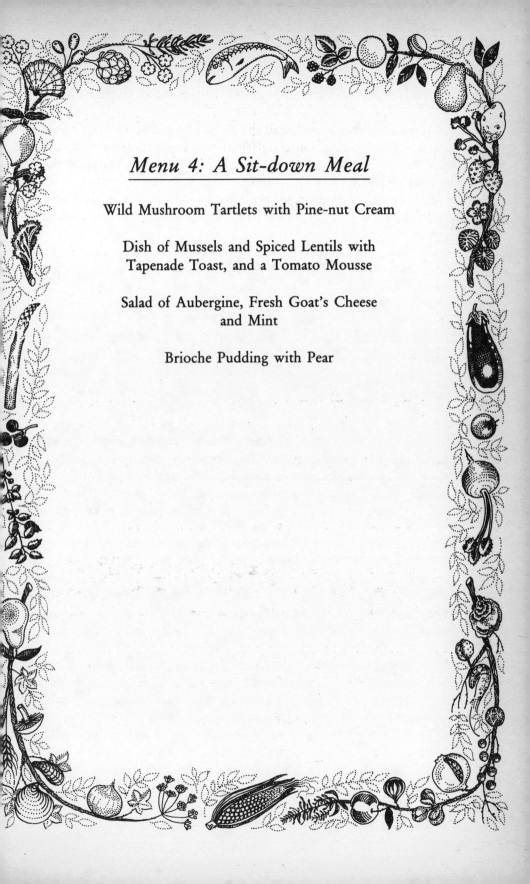

Menu 4: A Sit-down Meal

Wild Mushroom Tartlets with Pine-nut Cream

Dish of Mussels and Spiced Lentils with
Tapenade Toast, and a Tomato Mousse

Salad of Aubergine, Fresh Goat's Cheese
and Mint

Brioche Pudding with Pear

Wild Mushroom Tartlets with Pine-nut Cream

Of the 1,200 edible species of wild mushrooms to be found in Europe, the vast majority have eluded the would-be cultivator. Oyster mushrooms and shiitake mushrooms are exceptions, but they have failed to bring their true character and mystique with them from the wild. The Padi Straw mushroom is cultivated in the Far East, and it may be that soon we shall find 'honey fungus' packaged in neat plastic cartons stamped with a sell-by date. Dried wild mushrooms are fairly widely available, the most common of these being ceps and morels. Once reconstituted, they are both excellent used in soups, in stews or in conjunction with cultivated mushrooms. The morels offer the additional quality of plumping up to their original state when soaked; the ceps have to be sliced before they are dried. If buying dried ceps, look for ones which contain as much of their original shape as possible, not an assortment of fragments. To use dried mushrooms, soak them in hot water for 15 minutes, then strain the liquid through muslin or a fine-mesh sieve to remove any grit. The liquid can be used in a soup or sauce.

You may, of course, be one of those fortunates who have a mycologically-orientated local shop, in which case, for the exchange of a fair number of pennies, you can indulge in a feast of fresh chanterelles, *trompettes des morts*, ceps or morels. Becoming involved in the science of mycology enables us to take advantage of the rich offerings of our native woodlands and fields. Mycologist *extraordinaire* Antonio Carluccio (or mycophile or mycophagist as he calls himself), the proprietor of the Neal Street Restaurant, has transformed it into a mecca of these elusive fungi; during autumn days the menu reads like an ode to a wild mushroom. Signor Carluccio employs professional gatherers who scour the hills and woodlands to bring back a cornucopia of edible wild mushrooms. Caesar's mushroom, honey fungus, giant puffballs, chanterelles, ceps, shaggy ink-caps, cauliflower fungus and hedgehog fungus are just some of those to be found, but for the majority of us the experience of eating them remains a fantasy unless we happen to frequent Signor Carluccio's restaurant.

For the would-be mushroom-hunter, there are vast untapped harvests of these fruiting bodies to be had. Traditionally disregarded by the English, it remains a mystery to me that there are not clutches of entrepreneurial Italians buried in little huts deep in the English woods, running profitable export businesses. In reality, though, the export of wild mushrooms from the British Isles is a growing industry; and some restaurants now pick their own, or may be supplied by an enterprising picker.

In Trento in Italy one can hope to find up to thirty-five different species of edible mushroom for sale during the season. Inspectors may be appointed by the Government to vet the mushrooms before they are sold; in France during the season, chemists will inspect the fruits of your picking. Antonio Carluccio's book *A Passion for Mushrooms* is an excellent guide to inspire the uninitiated: illustrated with colour photographs, it deals with how to recognize edible and poisonous species of wild mushrooms, how to cook them, how to preserve them by drying, freezing, pickling or salting, and a field guide to picking and identifying them. It is worth equipping yourself with a couple of other good reference or guide books on the subject too, before starting out.

Tartlets

3 sheets filo pastry (approx.)	14 oz/400 g wild mushrooms
1 oz/30 g unsalted butter, melted	salt and pepper
1 clove garlic	1 tablespoon finely chopped flat-leaf parsley
3 tablespoons olive oil	

Pine-nut cream

1 oz/30 g dried porcini	1 dessertspoon brandy
2 oz/55 g pine-nuts	4 fl oz/115 ml double cream
	salt

To garnish

salad leaves	nut-oil vinaigrette (see p. 28)

Place the porcini in a bowl, cover them with boiling water and soak them for 15 minutes. Preheat the oven to 170°C/325°F/Gas 3.

Prepare the tartlet cases. Paint a sheet of filo pastry with melted butter, keeping the remaining sheets covered to avoid them drying out. Cut it into six squares and line two 4-in/10-cm tartlet cases with three squares each, so that the corners form petals. Repeat this process with the remaining sheets of filo. Bake the tartlets for 8-10 minutes or until they are golden.

Prepare the sauce by liquidizing the pine-nuts with the porcini and the liquid they have soaked in. Heat this in a small saucepan together with the brandy, cream and salt. Simmer the sauce for a couple of minutes, stirring occasionally until it thickens. The sauce should be thick, spoonable but thinner than mayonnaise.

Fifteen minutes before serving time, rub a frying-pan with the clove of garlic and heat a small amount of olive oil in it. When the oil is hot, cover the base of the pan with mushrooms, cook them for a few minutes, remove them to a bowl and season them. Cook the remaining mushrooms. Keep them warm in the oven. Just before serving, stir in the parsley.

While the mushrooms are cooking, warm the tartlet cases in the oven, and reheat the pine-nut cream if necessary.

To serve, spread the pine-nut cream on the base of the tartlet cases and fill them with mushrooms. Each plate can be garnished with a small clutch of salad leaves, dressed with a nut-oil vinaigrette.

Dish of Mussels and Spiced Lentils with Tapenade Toast, and a Tomato Mousse

Puy lentils, from le Puy in the Auvergne, are beautiful, tiny, marbled slate-green pellets which sadly lose their sheen and brightness as they cook, turning to a mundane khaki. But they retain their shape and have a better texture than the ordinary variety, which become pulpy on cooking. Currently they are the domain of the good deli; protected by 'Origine controlée', they are unlikely ever to become of such abundance as to elbow out their baser cousins.

Mousse

4 fl oz/115 ml double cream	*3 tablespoons tomato, peeled,*
4 fl oz/115 ml crème fraîche	*seeded, and diced (concassée)*
¼ sachet gelatine	*lemon juice*
2 teaspoons sun-dried tomato	*salt*
paste	

Lentils

8 fl oz/225 ml grape juice	½ teaspoon each of ground
10 oz/285 g Puy lentils	coriander and cumin
5 tablespoons olive oil vinaigrette	¾ teaspoon anchovy essence
(p. 28)	5 lb/2.3 kg mussels
1 teaspoon honey	

Croûtons

1 small stick French bread	olive oil

Tapenade

4 oz/115 g black olives, pitted	½ clove garlic
½ oz/15 g capers	1 tablespoon olive oil
pinch of thyme	black pepper
1 teaspoon brandy (optional)	

Prepare the tomato mousse some hours in advance. Whip together the double cream and *crème fraîche*. Dissolve the gelatine in a little boiling water and stir this into the cream. Gently fold in the sun-dried tomato paste, followed by the tomato concassée. Season the mousse with lemon juice and salt. Cover the mixture and put it in the fridge to set.

Boil the grape juice until it reduces to a couple of tablespoons of syrup. Simmer the lentils in water for about 25 minutes or until they are cooked. Strain them and pour water through them until it runs clear. Mix the lentils with the vinaigrette, honey, spices, reduced grape juice and anchovy essence.

Scrub the mussels, discarding any that are broken or do not close tightly when tapped. Remove the beards. Steam the mussels open in a large covered saucepan over a high heat, cooking them for about 5 minutes. Shake the pan occasionally. Remove the mussels from their shells. Strain the remaining liquor through muslin into a small pan and reduce it until only a few tablespoons remain. Add the mussels to the lentils with about half the reduced mussel liquor, being guided by taste.

To make the croûtons, slice the French bread thinly and fry in plenty of olive oil in a frying-pan. Cool on parchment paper.

To make the tapenade, purée the olives, capers, thyme, brandy and garlic in a food processor, adding the olive oil in a thin stream at the end. Season with black pepper.

To serve the dish, reheat the lentils. Spread the croûtons liberally with the tapenade. Place a pile of lentils on each plate with a quenelle of tomato mousse, and surround the lentils with the croûtons.

Salad of Aubergine, Fresh Goat's Cheese and Mint

Serve this salad at room temperature but prepare it as close to the time of serving as possible.

2 medium aubergines	4 tablespoons white wine
salt	black pepper
olive oil	4 oz/115 g fresh goat's cheese
2 tablespoons sherry vinegar	handful of mint leaves

Cut the aubergines into ¼-in/0.75-cm slices. Salt the slices liberally on both sides and leave them for 1 hour, then rinse and dry them. Heat a small amount of olive oil in a frying-pan, and when it is hot fry the slices in batches to a deep brown.

If the pan has become very hot, allow it to cool for a few minutes, then deglaze it with the vinegar and white wine, which should reduce by half; pour this over the aubergine. Allow it to cool to room temperature. Grind black pepper over the dish. Break the goat's cheese up into roughly-shaped cubes and arrange them on the aubergine. Reserving a quarter of the mint leaves, coarsely chop the rest and scatter them over the dish. Garnish with the remaining leaves. Dribble over more olive oil when serving.

Brioche Pudding with Pear

2 tablespoons raisins	4 tablespoons sugar
Poire William liqueur	9 fl oz/250 ml milk
5 oz/140 g brioche	9 fl oz/250 ml double cream
3 oz/85 g butter	2 William pears, firm but ripe
3 eggs	

Place the raisins in a small bowl or cup, cover them with liqueur and allow them to absorb it for a couple of hours. Tear the brioche into pieces. Heat half the butter in a frying-pan and cook half the pieces of brioche until they are golden on all sides. Cook the remaining brioche in the same fashion, using the rest of the butter. Whisk the eggs and pass them through a sieve, then whisk in the sugar and add the milk and cream.

Peel and core the pears, and cut them into thin slices. Arrange the brioche, pear and raisins in a gratin dish or casserole and pour the custard over. Sprinkle 2 tablespoons of the liqueur over the custard (some will remain from soaking the raisins). Craggy peaks of brioche should show through the custard. Bake the pudding for 30-35 minutes at 180°C/350°F/Gas 4. The custard in the centre should be slightly *baveuse*.

Menu 5: A Sit-down Meal

Fennel and Almond Soup

Fish Pie with Sautéed Cucumber

Leeks Braised in White Wine

Creamed Pumpkin Baked with Corn

Pavlova with Hot Apples and Spices

Fennel and Almond Soup

2 large bulbs fennel	2 pints/1.1 litres vegetable stock
2 sticks celery	2 oz/55 g ground almonds
2 carrots	1 tablespoon Pernod
2 shallots	salt and white pepper
1 oz/30 g butter	

Finely chop the vegetables. Melt the butter in a large saucepan and sweat them for 5 minutes. Add the vegetable stock and simmer the soup for a few minutes until the vegetables are tender. Purée the soup and return it to the pan.

Add the ground almonds and season the soup. Cook until it thickens. Stir in the Pernod. The soup could be decorated with a julienne of carrot, sweated in a little butter for a few minutes.

Fish Pie with Sautéed Cucumber

People who have taken a course in transcendental meditation often comment that during the introductory session the instructor takes you to sublime depths of relaxation and peace of mind, and that thereafter every meditation is spent trying to recreate that original sublime state without ever quite achieving it.

This particular fish pie has a similar refrain. I first made it for dinner on a boat moored in a picturesque curve on the River Thames, just outside Henley, one late summer evening. The assembled company all declared that it was undoubtedly the best fish pie they had ever eaten, so the following morning I carefully annotated every detail of it. This recipe is the nearest I can come to the original dish − still not quite as good, though I suspect that seasoned with some damp river air, a dramatic pink and orange sky, many bottles of good wine, mosquitoes and clouds of Monte Cristo cigar smoke, once again it might blush in the face of flattery.

It is always refreshing to have an entrenched belief challenged and proved wrong, particularly when it comes as a pleasant surprise. Olive oil and cream were two ingredients that for years I had avoided marrying in dishes − this potato purée, which combines olive oil and cream, is undeniably the most delicious of potato purées and confirms the unlikely affinity of these two ingredients. The olive oil should come through loud and clear, so use the amounts given for guidance only. A large dollop of this purée, accompanied by warm char-grilled vegetables sprinkled with herbs and more olive oil dribbled over, scores highly as recherché snack food.

Any firm-fleshed white fish can be used, whatever is fresh and available. Sea bass makes it a king of pies; sadly there is no season of cheap abundance for this fish, although endeavours currently under way to farm it may soon alter this. A mixture of monkfish, scallops and cod would be an excellent alternative to the fish suggested below.

Potato purée

2½ lb/1.1 kg floury potatoes	3 fl oz/85 ml extra virgin olive oil
1½ fl oz/45 ml double cream	freshly ground white pepper, salt

Cucumber

1 large cucumber	½ oz/15 g butter
salt	

Fish

1½ lb/675 g firm-fleshed white fish, filleted: halibut, gurnard, brill, turbot, sea bass	2 tablespoons vermouth
	¼ pint/150 ml double cream
	1 oz/30 g sorrel
2 pints/1.1 litres fish stock	knife tip tarragon, finely chopped
1 oz/30 g butter	salt and freshly ground white pepper
¾ oz/20 g flour	

Peel the potatoes and put them to boil until they are well cooked, about 30 minutes. Peel the cucumber, slice it finely, sprinkle the slices with salt and put them aside on a plate.

Cut the fish fillets into pieces. Heat the fish stock and simmer the fish for 3 minutes, then remove it to a bowl. Reduce the stock to ¼ pint/150 ml. Make a roux with the butter and flour. Traditionally, equal quantities of flour and butter are used, but a touch less flour makes it considerably easier to blend in the liquid without stubborn lumps remaining. Cook the roux for 1 minute, then blend in the fish stock, the vermouth and then the cream. Make a chiffonade (p. 13) of sorrel and add this to the sauce; continue to cook it until it turns a dull green. Add the tarragon and season the sauce.

Strain the potatoes and allow any surface water to evaporate. Pass them through a mouli-légumes, or mash them and press them through a sieve. Beat in the cream, olive oil and seasoning.

Rinse the cucumber and drain it on kitchen paper. Melt the butter in a frying-pan and gently cook the slices on both sides until they are transparent and flaccid.

Drain and discard any liquid exuded by the fish; combine the sauce and the fish and place in a casserole or deep pie dish. Lay the cucumber over and spread the potato on top, forking the surface into furrows.

Cook the pie in the oven at 180°C/350°F/Gas 4 for 30-35 minutes until the surface is brown and crisp.

Leeks Braised in White Wine

This is adapted from a recipe in Jane Grigson's *Vegetable Book*, called German Leeks and Wine. It scores highly for simplicity, it is one of the best ways of cooking leeks, and they escape the slimy fate of many boiled ones.

1½ lb/675 g leeks	5 fl oz/150 ml white wine
2 oz/55 g butter	salt and pepper

Trim the root of each leek and cut off the dark green shoots. Remove the outer layer and rinse the surface. Slice them ¼ in/0.75 cm thick and rinse them well in a sieve.

Place all the ingredients in a saucepan, bring the liquid to the boil, cover the pan and cook over a low heat for 25-30 minutes. Remove the lid. The leeks should be coated in a butter sauce, but if there is liquid remaining, turn up the heat and continue cooking until it has all but evaporated.

Creamed Pumpkin Baked with Corn

Autumn shops are filled with gourds of all sizes, colours and shapes. The very largest and very smallest are proudly put on display. For an informal occasion, family or good friends only, cut the top off a pumpkin and scoop out the seeds and surface fibres. Fill the cavity with cream, Gruyère and croûtons. Replace the top and return the pumpkin to a hot oven for an hour or more, depending on its size. Be sure it does not overcook and collapse when you remove it. Lift off the lid and scoop the flesh and creamy fondue into a saucepan. With silent reverence take a spoon and eat this stuff.

1½ lb/675 g pumpkin	salt and pepper
2 heads of corn	nutmeg
4 fl oz/115 ml double cream	

Remove skin, seeds and evident fibres from the pumpkin and thinly slice it. Completely cook the corn on the cob in a large pan of water, then slice off the kernels.

Preheat the oven to 180°C/350°F/Gas 4. Place the pumpkin and corn together in a gratin dish. Season the cream with salt, pepper and nutmeg, and pour it over the vegetables. Cover the dish with foil and place it in the oven for 20 minutes; remove the foil, stir the vegetables and cook them for another 20 minutes until the surface is brown in places.

Pavlova with Hot Apples and Spices

The recipe for this marshmallow-like meringue was passed on to me by Heidi Lascelles, custodian of the country's largest cookery library at Books for Cooks in Notting Hill. Understandably it is a great favourite with children. This recipe starts with a deep base of meringue, topped with *crème fraîche* and whipped cream. Hot apples and grapes coated in a butterscotch sauce are placed on top of this, causing the surface cream to melt into a warm sweet river, leaving a layer of cool thick cream beneath.

Meringue

6 egg whites	1 tablespoon cornflour
12 oz/340 g caster sugar	1 teaspoon white wine vinegar

Spiced fruit

¾ lb/340 g apples	2 tablespoons honey
¼ lb/115 g seedless grapes	¼ teaspooon cinnamon
1 oz/30 g butter	pinch ground cloves

To assemble

5 fl oz/150 ml double cream	*5 fl oz/150 ml* crème fraîche

Cut a circle of baking parchment to fit an 8-in/20-cm springform cake tin. Preheat the oven to its highest setting.

The egg whites need to be at room temperature. Whip them until they start to stiffen. Whisk in the caster sugar a few tablespoons at a time, whisking well between each addition. Whisk in the cornflour and vinegar. You should have a glossy, stiff meringue that peaks when you lift a spoon out of it. It is quite stable and will retain this body for up to an hour.

Rinse the inside of the cake tin with water, place the parchment circle on the base of the tin and rinse it again. Spoon the meringue into the tin, smoothing the surface. Place it in the oven and either turn the oven off and leave the meringue overnight or turn it down to its lowest setting and cook it for a couple of hours, making sure the surface does not start to brown.

Peel and core the apples and slice them into crescents; remove the grapes from the vine, leaving them whole. Melt the butter in a frying-pan and add the honey and spices. Cook the sauce for a minute or two until it forms a smooth butterscotch, then add the fruit and cook it over a low heat for 10 minutes. If the fruit exudes juices, thinning the sauce, remove it and reduce the sauce. Allow it to cool for a few minutes.

Whip the *crème fraîche* and double cream together until stiff.

Remove the springform collar from the meringue, slice off and discard the hard surface and invert it on to a plate. Spread the cream over the meringue and place the apples in the centre. Serve the dessert in large wedges. It may be easier to cut the meringue before assembling it, adding the cream and fruit on the individual plates.

The meringue could also be made in a straight-sided terrine and cut into thick slices, the cream and fruit placed on top.

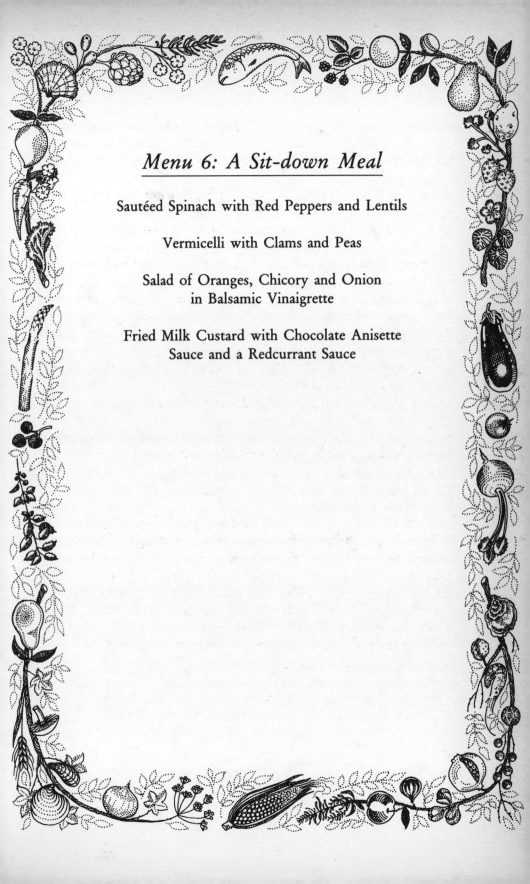

Menu 6: A Sit-down Meal

Sautéed Spinach with Red Peppers and Lentils

Vermicelli with Clams and Peas

Salad of Oranges, Chicory and Onion
in Balsamic Vinaigrette

Fried Milk Custard with Chocolate Anisette
Sauce and a Redcurrant Sauce

Sautéed Spinach with Red Peppers and Lentils

Cibo in west London, along with a handful of other restaurants, vies for premiership in serving the best authentic Italian food in London. This is a starter to be found on the menu there.

3 red peppers	salt and pepper
2½ oz/70 g Puy lentils	1 clove garlic
olive oil	1½ lb/675 g young spinach leaves

Roast, skin and deseed the peppers according to the instructions on p. 108. Cut them into strips.

Boil the lentils in water for 25 minutes, then drain them and pour boiling water through them until it runs clear. Dress them with olive oil and season them. Return them to the pan and keep them warm over a low heat.

Finely chop the garlic. Wash the spinach, remove any tough stalks, and dry the leaves well. Heat a little olive oil in a large saucepan. Add some of the chopped garlic, and moments later throw in some spinach leaves and toss them until they are coated with oil and starting to wilt. Cover the pan and cook them for 1 minute. Remove them to a bowl and season them. Cook the remaining spinach in the same fashion.

Heat the pepper strips in the pan in which the spinach has cooked. Take six plates and place some of the spinach on each one, arrange some pepper strips over it and strew the lentils over.

Vermicelli with Clams and Peas

Of the six or seven varieties of clam to be found in a fishmonger's, the most common is the small Venus clam. Sweet and tender, these clams are ideal for this recipe, though a larger bivalve could be used if necessary.

3 lb/1.4 kg Venus clams	1 onion
5 fl oz/150 ml white wine	1 clove garlic
2 pints/1.1 litres double-strength	1 sachet of saffron (⅛ teaspoon)
fish stock	salt and cayenne pepper
4 tablespoons olive oil	10 oz/285 g petit pois
8 oz/225 g vermicelli	handful of mint

Clean the clams according to the instructions on p. 55, taking care that they soak for an adequate period of time. Place them with the wine in a saucepan, cover the pot tightly and steam them open. Large clams can be stubborn in opening, which places the open ones in danger of being overcooked. Remove any recalcitrant clams to a small saucepan with a little of the fish stock and steam them for a few minutes longer. Strain the liquor through muslin or a sieve lined with kitchen paper, and add it to the fish stock. Shell the clams, reserving a few unshelled ones as a garnish.

Heat 2 tablespoons of olive oil in a large saucepan or casserole. Break the vermicelli into 3-in lengths and sauté it until it turns golden. Turn it constantly, using two long-handled spoons. Set aside.

Finely chop the onion and garlic, add another 2 tablespoons of oil to the pan and sweat them for 10 minutes over a low heat until they are cooked but not coloured. Add the fish stock, saffron and cayenne pepper and bring to the boil. (If you are making this in the spring, using fresh peas, add them at this stage.) Add the vermicelli, cover the pot tightly and cook for 5 minutes until it is done. If you are using frozen petit pois, add them now and bring the stew back to the boil. Add the shelled clams and heat them through. Adjust the seasoning.

Finely chop the mint. Ladle the stew into bowls, garnish it with the reserved unshelled clams and sprinkle some chopped mint over.

Salad of Oranges, Chicory and Onion in Balsamic Vinaigrette

If you are making this salad in the spring, take advantage of the availability of blood oranges.

Balsamic vinegar is made in Modena from the white Trebbiano grape. The grapes are harvested late; they are pressed and the must is run off as though making wine. The must is filtered before any degree of fermentation commences. It is then boiled to achieve the desired concentration, which depends on the sugar level, the vintage and house practice. The must is filtered again, cooled and poured into oak casks. This procedure is known as 'topping up'. The vinegar is then aged in successively smaller casks, usually of chestnut, cherry, ash and mulberry, as it increases in concentration. Traditional balsamic vinegar must have been aged for at least ten years. Commercially produced balsamic vinegar will be a blend of vinegars aged for different lengths of time. The more superior the vinegar, the greater proportion of old vinegar it is likely to contain. Used infrequently and with caution, it is worth keeping an extremely good one — I have found the vinegars on sale in supermarkets hopelessly inadequate.

Salad

4 small oranges	½ red onion, cut vertically
3 heads of chicory, or 2 large ones	1 bulb of fennel

Vinaigrette

2 teaspoons balsamic vinegar	6 tablespoons extra virgin olive
salt and pepper	oil

Segment the oranges by cutting off the skin and pith, and running a knife between each segment to remove the orange flesh, leaving the pith which separates them. Separate the chicory leaves. Thinly slice the onion into crescents.

Discard the outer sheaves of the fennel bulb, and any shoots. Slice the bulb into crescents not longer than 2 in/5 cm. Blanch these for 1-2 minutes and plunge them into cold water.

Arrange the orange, chicory, onion and fennel together on a platter. Whisk the balsamic vinegar with the salt and pepper, add the oil, and pour the dressing over the salad.

Fried Milk Custard with Chocolate Anisette Sauce and a Redcurrant Sauce

Fried milk custard seemed such an unlikely item on the menu of an Italian restaurant that it demanded attention. What arrived was a thick slice of custard deep-fried, with a thin crisp shell and a molten inside of hot custard cream. This dessert is also typically Spanish.

Any of the Mediterranean anise-flavoured drinks or liqueurs can be used here. They differ slightly in taste, depending on whether the seeds of star anise or aniseed flavour the drink.

Milk custard

1 pint/600 ml milk	4½ oz/125 g plain flour
1-in stick cinnamon	6 oz/170 g caster sugar
2 strips lemon peel	2 egg yolks
5 oz/140 g butter	

Chocolate anisette sauce

5 oz/140 g bitter chocolate	1½ dessertspoons Pernod or other
8 fl oz/225 ml single cream	pastis

Redcurrant sauce

6 oz/170 g redcurrant jelly	3 dessertspoons lemon juice

For frying

oil	beaten egg
flour	breadcrumbs

Prepare the custard by heating the milk and infusing it with the cinnamon stick and lemon peel for 15 minutes. Melt the butter, add the flour and cook the roux for 1-2 minutes. Strain the milk and incorporate it into the roux, then stir in the sugar. Cook the custard for a few minutes to take away any floury taste. Remove the custard to a bowl, allow it to cool slightly and beat in the egg yolks.

Select a tin or mould which will hold the custard to a depth of approximately 1 in/2.5 cm and brush it lightly with a flavourless oil. Press the custard into the mould, smoothing the surface. Cover it with cling-film, allow it to cool and then chill it. Cut it into squares, diamonds or wedges, allowing two per person.

To make the chocolate anisette sauce, melt the chocolate in a double boiler, stir in the cream and Pernod and heat the sauce through.

Heat the redcurrant jelly with the lemon juice and pass it through a sieve.

Heat a pan of oil until it is hot but not smoking. Dip the custard pieces into the flour, then the beaten egg and then breadcrumbs. Deep-fry them to a deep gold.

The sauces should be hot but not boiling. Take six plates and spoon the chocolate sauce between them. Place a generous teaspoon of redcurrant sauce to the side. Place the milk custards on top of the sauce.

Winter

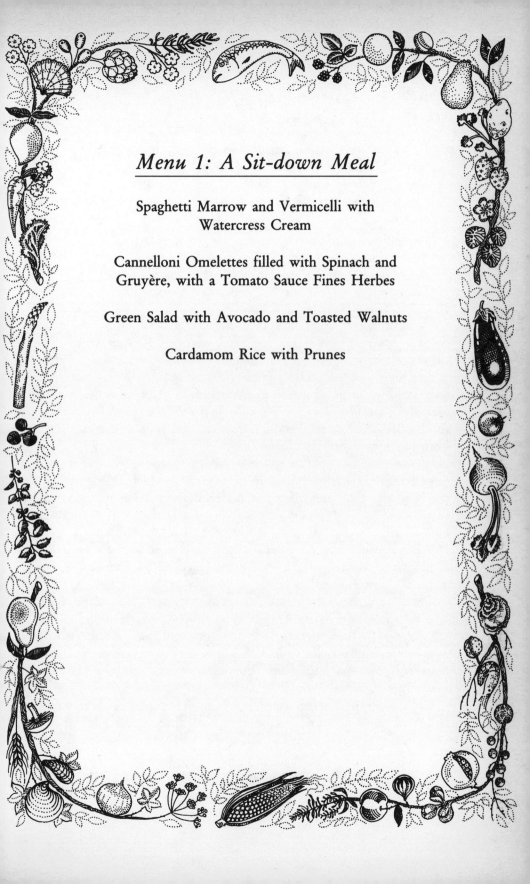

Menu 1: A Sit-down Meal

Spaghetti Marrow and Vermicelli with
Watercress Cream

Cannelloni Omelettes filled with Spinach and
Gruyère, with a Tomato Sauce Fines Herbes

Green Salad with Avocado and Toasted Walnuts

Cardamom Rice with Prunes

Spaghetti Marrow and Vermicelli with Watercress Cream

The oblong spaghetti marrow which forks into thin, crunchy strands of vegetable spaghetti is a delight. It can be tossed with any number of rich spaghetti sauces or served as a gratin. It requires thorough draining after it has been spaghettied, but can be reheated if required.

2 spaghetti marrow	⅛ pint/75 ml white wine
1 bunch watercress	1 tablespoon lemon juice
3 level tablespoons crème fraîche	4 oz/115 g butter
salt and pepper	3 oz/85 g vermicelli

Set a large saucepan or casserole of water to boil. Run a skewer through each spaghetti marrow and boil for 30 minutes in all, turning them over after 15 minutes.

Pick over the watercress, removing any tough stems. Reserve a large handful of good leaves to garnish each plate. Boil the watercress for 3 minutes. Drain it well. Purée it with the *crème fraîche* in a food processor. Season the sauce with salt and pepper. Reheat it and keep it warm over a low heat.

Prepare a lemon butter sauce by reducing the wine and lemon juice by half. Cut the butter into cubes and whisk it in piece by piece, working on and off the heat as necessary. Remove the sauce from the heat and season it with salt. Either keep it warm in a bain-marie or reheat it very gently when it is required.

Bring another pan of water to the boil and cook the vermicelli. Drain it and toss it with the watercress sauce. Allow it to absorb the sauce for a minute or two.

Cut the spaghetti marrow in half vertically and remove the seeds with a large spoon. Working over a sieve, run a fork from one end of the marrow to the other, forking the flesh into spaghetti. Press out as much moisture as possible with a spoon or potato masher. Dress the vegetable spaghetti with the lemon butter and adjust the seasoning.

On heated plates, place a small pile of the vermicelli in watercress cream in the centre and surround it with three small piles of the vegetable spaghetti. Garnish each plate with watercress leaves.

Cannelloni Omelettes filled with Spinach and Gruyère, with a Tomato Sauce Fines Herbes

Sauce

2 lb/0.9 kg ripe tomatoes	salt
2 oz/55 g butter	fines herbes, *finely chopped*
1 small onion, halved	*(chervil, chives, parsley,*
¼ teaspoon sugar	*tarragon)*

Omelettes

6 eggs	3 tablespoons finely chopped
salt and pepper	parsley
	½ oz/15 g butter

Filling

3 × 10 oz/285 g packets frozen	3 tablespoons crème fraîche
spinach, or equivalent of fresh	salt and pepper
4 oz/115 g Gruyère, grated	1 egg, beaten

Make the sauce first. Slice the tomatoes, place them in a tightly covered pan over a very low heat, and cook them for 30-40 minutes, until they collapse. Purée the tomatoes and pass them through a sieve back into the pan. Add the butter, onion and sugar and cook the sauce at a steady simmer for 30 minutes. Remove the onion and season the sauce with salt.

Prepare the omelettes by beating the eggs well and passing them through a sieve. Season them with salt and pepper and add the parsley. Melt a small knob of butter in a 6-in crêpe pan — when the foam subsides, coat the base of the pan with 2 tablespoons of egg as if making a crêpe. Turn the omelette after 30 seconds and cook for a further 15 seconds. Turn it out on to a plate. Repeat the process, using more butter if required. You will require two omelettes per person.

If using frozen spinach, defrost and drain it well. Combine it with the Gruyère, *crème fraîche* and seasoning, and bind the mixture with the beaten egg.

Preheat the oven to 170°C/325°F/Gas 3. Butter a gratin dish. Cut two opposite sides off each omelette. Place a large spoonful of the filling in a cylinder along one of the rough edges and roll the omelettes up to form cannelloni. Repeat with the rest of the omelettes. Place them side by side in the gratin dish. Cover the dish with foil and heat it for 15 minutes in the oven.

Reheat the sauce and the plates. Place two cannelloni on each plate, pour over some sauce and sprinkle with a few *fines herbes*.

Green Salad with Avocado and Toasted Walnuts

mixture of salad greens to feed 6 people

Dressing

1 dessertspoon sherry vinegar	4 dessertspoons walnut oil
¼ teaspoon mustard	4 dessertspoons arachide
¼ teaspoon salt	(groundnut) oil

Salad

1 large hass avocado	2 handfuls walnut pieces
1 tablespoon walnut oil	

Make the dressing by whisking the vinegar with the mustard and salt until the salt dissolves. Whisk in the oils.

Wash and dry the salad greens and place them in a bowl. Halve the avovado, peel it and cut it into thin slices and add it to the salad.

Heat the tablespoon of walnut oil in a small saucepan or frying-pan and cook the walnuts until they have toasted to a light gold. Cool the nuts for a minute or so, then add the dressing to the pan and pour the contents on to the salad. Toss it and serve warm.

Cardamom Rice with Prunes

I find Whitworth's stoned prunes the best for this recipe. Widely available, they closely resemble the Agen prunes, which would be ideal.

Rice

5 oz/140 g risotto rice	*2 oz/55 g sugar*
3/4 pint/450 ml milk	*15 cardamom pods*
1 oz/30 g butter	

Custard

3 egg yolks	*11 fl oz/300 ml milk*
2½ oz/70 g caster sugar	*5 fl oz/150 ml double cream*

Prunes

3 oz/85 g sugar	*2-in/5-cm cinnamon stick*
3 fl oz/85 ml Armagnac plus 3	*1 bay leaf*
* dessertspoons*	*3/4 lb/340 g stoned prunes (no*
1 vanilla pod, slit	* need to soak variety)*

Boil the rice for 5 minutes and drain it. In a flameproof casserole on top of the stove bring the milk, butter and sugar to the boil; add the cardamom pods and stir in the rice. Bring it back to a simmer, then cover the casserole with a circle of buttered greaseproof paper and the casserole lid. Preheat the oven to 200°C/400°F/Gas 6, place the rice in the oven and turn it down to 130°C/225°F/Gas ½. Cook the rice for 40 minutes, until it has absorbed all the milk. Remove the cardamom pods and cool the rice.

Meanwhile make the custard. Beat together the egg yolks and the sugar until the mixture is pale yellow. Bring the milk to the boil, beat it into the egg mixture and return it to the pan over a very low heat. Cook until the mixture thickens or just coats the back of a spoon. Do not allow it to boil. Strain into a jug or bowl.

When both the custard and the rice have cooled to room temperature, combine them and stir in the cream. Chill the mixture for several hours or overnight; the desired consistency should be that of Ambrosia tinned rice.

Prepare a syrup with the sugar, 3 fl oz/85 ml of Armagnac, the vanilla pod, cinnamon stick, bay leaf and 1 pint of water and simmer for 10 minutes. Add the prunes and simmer them, covered, for 30 minutes. Remove them to a bowl and add the remaining Armagnac to the syrup. Pour the liquor over the prunes and allow them to cool. Chill them, leaving the spices in the bowl.

Serve the prunes and rice together in bowls.

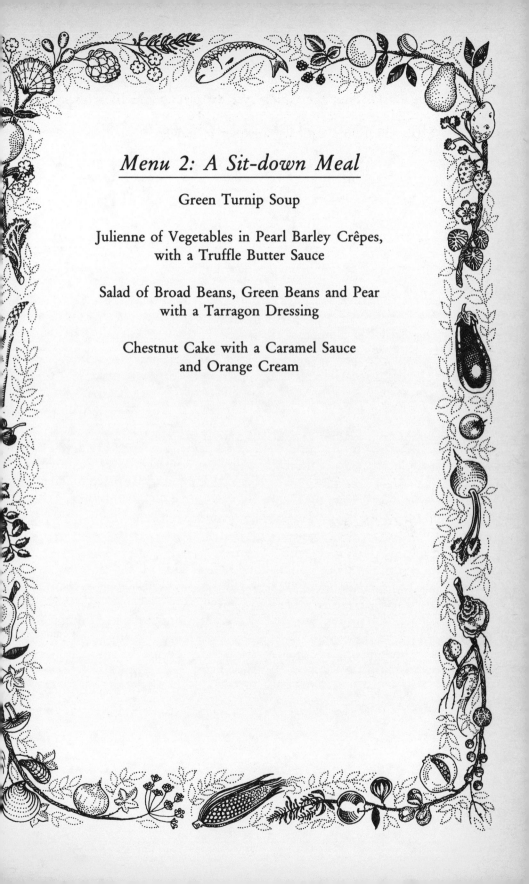

Menu 2: A Sit-down Meal

Green Turnip Soup

Julienne of Vegetables in Pearl Barley Crêpes,
with a Truffle Butter Sauce

Salad of Broad Beans, Green Beans and Pear
with a Tarragon Dressing

Chestnut Cake with a Caramel Sauce
and Orange Cream

Green Turnip Soup

In the spring this soup can be made with turnips and turnip greens, which make it slightly bitter; I personally like this, but it can be toned down by substituting half of the greens with spinach. As an autumn soup, use spinach and watercress in place of turnip greens.

Turnip greens, or *broccoletti di rape*, are a favourite spring vegetable in Rome. They made a début in the Portobello Road market this last spring, and traders seemed astonished at the speed with which they were snapped up by shoppers, so with luck they may also become a feature of spring markets here.

Cook the older greens like any other member of the cabbage family, and dress them with olive oil and a little crushed garlic. Younger leaves are especially good wilted in butter with a pinch of sugar, salt and pepper.

1½ lb/675 g turnips	*¾ lb/340 g turnip greens, and/or*
2½ oz/70 g butter	*spinach and watercress*
sugar	*1½ pints/900 ml vegetable stock*
salt and pepper	*lemon juice*
	double cream

Peel and quarter the turnips. Place them in a pan with 1½ oz/45 g of butter and a teaspoon each of sugar and salt, just cover them with water and cook them, covered, for 15 minutes. Remove the lid and continue cooking to evaporate the remaining liquid; sweat the turnips for a few minutes in the residual butter.

Pick over and wash the greens. Heat a knob of butter in a frying-pan, throw in some greens and cook them until they wilt, then remove them to a bowl and season with a pinch of sugar and salt. Discard any liquid in the pan and cook the remaining greens the same way.

Purée the turnips with the greens and some stock in a liquidizer, and return the soup to the pan. Add the remaining stock and reheat the soup; season it with salt, pepper and a squeeze of lemon juice. Add a swirl of cream to each bowl as it is served.

The soup is at its best immediately it is made — when reheated it loses its freshness and colour.

Julienne of Vegetables in Pearl Barley Crêpes, with a Truffle Butter Sauce

While at their best straight from the pan, these crêpes can be prepared in advance and reheated, covered with foil, in a low oven. The vegetable julienne can be prepared well in advance too.

Crêpes

2 oz/55 g pearl barley	1 tablespoon fine old sherry
4 oz/115 g plain flour	good pinch of salt
1 egg	pinch of sugar
1 egg yolk	2 dessertspoons olive oil
½ pint/300 ml milk	

Sauce

2 walnut-sized truffles	9 oz/255 g butter
1 shallot	truffle oil or juice
10 fl oz/275 ml white wine	salt

Vegetables

4 medium carrots (approx. 6 oz/ 170 g)	2 small courgettes (approx. 6 oz/ 170 g)
2 inner sheaves of fennel	2 shallots
2 sticks of celery heart	

Boil the pearl barley in water for 45 minutes, then strain it and reserve it in a bowl. Make a pancake batter by whisking together all the other crêpe ingredients except the olive oil. Allow the batter to stand for an hour; add the pearl barley, then stir in the olive oil.

Cut the vegetables into juliennes 2 in/5 cm long. Keep the courgettes separate from the other vegetables. Prepare a julienne of the truffles.

Minutely dice the shallot for the sauce. Place it in a small saucepan with the wine and reduce to a couple of tablespoons. Cut the butter into pieces and whisk it in, working on and off a low heat as necessary. Flavour the sauce with truffle oil and season it with salt. Keep it warm or reheat it over a very low flame when it is needed.

Brush a 6-in/15-cm crêpe pan with olive oil and heat it. Thinly coat the base of the pan with batter, dispersing the barley as evenly as possible. Turn the crêpe when the upper side appears dry and pitted.

Blanch the carrot, fennel, celery and shallot julienne for 2 minutes, adding the courgette after 1 minute. Drain it well, dress it with a little of the butter sauce and season it.

Place some of the vegetable julienne in each pancake and form it into a cone. Spoon some of the butter sauce on to heated plates and place two crêpes on each one. Scatter the truffle julienne over the sauce.

Salad of Broad Beans, Green Beans and Pear with a Tarragon Dressing

Dressing

1 dessertspoon tarragon vinegar	1 level teaspoon tarragon, finely
¼ teaspoon salt	chopped
¼ teaspoon mustard	4 dessertspoons arachide
	(groundnut) oil
	4 dessertspoons olive oil

Salad

1 head chicory	4 oz/115 g dwarf green beans
1 green lettuce, or mixture of	1 large ripe pear
green leaves	chervil fronds
6 oz/170 g broad beans	

To make the dressing, whisk together the vinegar, salt, mustard and tarragon until the salt dissolves. Whisk in the oils.

Halve the chicory lengthwise and cut each half into thin strips. Prepare the lettuce, tearing it into pieces. If using frozen broad beans, defrost them, skin them and then boil them for 2 minutes. Cut the tails off the green beans and boil them for 2 minutes, then plunge them into cold water. Peel and core the pear and slice it thinly from top to bottom.

Toss the chicory, salad greens and green beans with the vinaigrette in a bowl and arrange them on a large platter. Scatter the broad beans over. Tuck the pear slices into the salad. Garnish with chervil fronds.

Chestnut Cake with a Caramel Sauce and Orange Cream

I have in my possession a much treasured first edition of Elizabeth David's *French Country Cooking*, illustrated by John Minton. The intact cover is a line drawing of a country kitchen, a château visible in the distance from the door leading outside, roughly coloured in with ochre, terracotta and blue. The section on sweets opens opposite an illustration of a baroque ball in progress, dining-table to the fore, groaning under the weight of silver, lavish displays of fruit and high-rise desserts crowned with grapes. On an adjacent table punch-bowl and glasses sit under a chandelier while couples waltz in the distance. The page opposite sports this recipe for Marrons à la Lyonnaise. The embellishment of caramel sauce and orange cream is my own.

Perhaps the designation 'cake' is a trifle misleading here. This is a dessert, fairly solid in texture and not the light and crumbly confection you might associate with tea-time. It is best eaten within hours of being made; it does not keep well even overnight.

Cake

1 lb/450 g tin unsweetened chestnut purée	3 oz/85 g butter, melted
2 cloves, ground	3 eggs
4 oz/115 g caster sugar	1 tablespoon brandy

Caramel

8 oz/225 g sugar	8 fl oz/225 ml water

Orange cream

½ pint/300 ml double cream	zest of 1 orange, finely chopped
few drops orange essence	

Combine the chestnut purée, cloves and sugar in a food processor. Add the melted butter. Separate the eggs and beat the egg yolks into the mixture; add the brandy. Stiffly beat the egg whites and fold them in. Pour the mixture into an 8-in/20-cm buttered springform cake tin, or one with a removable collar. Preheat the oven to 180°C/350°F/Gas 4 and bake the cake for 40 minutes or until it has set.

To make the caramel, boil the 8 oz/225 g of sugar with ¼ pint/150 ml of water until it turns a toffee-apple gold. Remove the pan to the sink and carefully add another 3 fl oz/85 ml of cold water. If the caramel is slow to dissolve, return it to a low heat. Cool the sauce and then chill it − it will thicken as it cools.

Whip the cream with the orange essence, and fold in the zest.

Serve the cake cut in slices with a spoon of cream to the side and the caramel trickled over both.

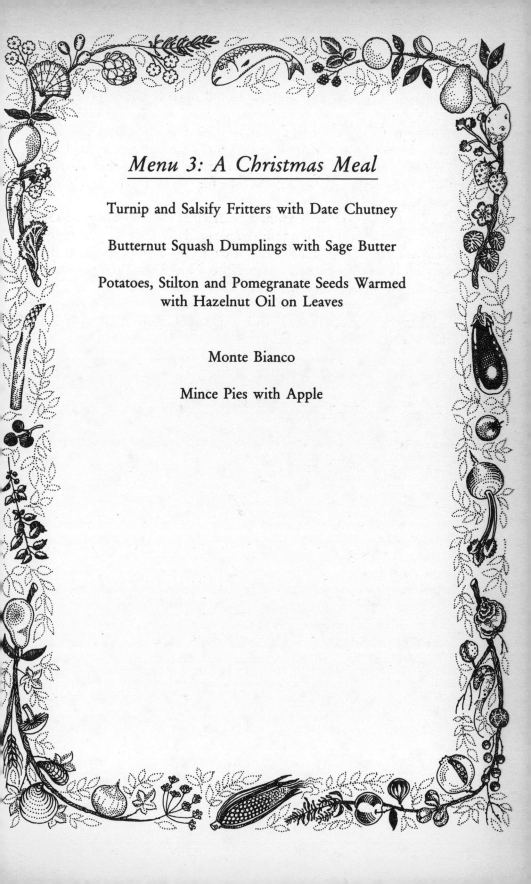

Menu 3: A Christmas Meal

Turnip and Salsify Fritters with Date Chutney

Butternut Squash Dumplings with Sage Butter

Potatoes, Stilton and Pomegranate Seeds Warmed
with Hazelnut Oil on Leaves

Monte Bianco

Mince Pies with Apple

Turnip and Salsify Fritters with Date Chutney

Chutney

8 oz/225 g dates, stoned	½ oz/15 g caster sugar
1 small onion	knife tip cayenne pepper
2 pieces preserved ginger	5 fl oz/150 ml wine vinegar
4 oz/115 g dried apricots, soaked	1 level teaspoon salt
1½ oz/45 g sultanas	

Batter

2 eggs	7 fl oz/200 ml milk
4 oz/115 g plain flour	½ teaspoon salt
2 tablespoons arachide (ground- nut) oil	

Fritters

14 oz/400 g thin salsify	1 lb/450 g medium-sized
½ lemon	turnips
1 teaspoon flour	vegetable oil for frying

First make the chutney. Chop the dates, onion, ginger and apricots. Place all the ingredients together in a pan and just cover them with water. Gently simmer the mixture for 50 minutes, interrupting it occasionally to make sure it is not sticking on the bottom of the pan. Keep a particularly careful eye during the last 10 minutes as it dries out; stop cooking it while there is still some liquid evident.

Separate the eggs. Whisk together the yolks, flour, oil, milk and salt till you have a smooth paste. Just before frying the fritters, whisk the egg whites until they are stiff and fold them into the batter.

Wearing rubber gloves to avoid staining your hands, peel the salsify, cut it into 2-in/5-cm lengths and immediately place them in a bowl of acidulated water. Boil them for 10 minutes in a pan of water containing the lemon juice and the flour, which will keep them white. Plunge them into cold water until they are required. Peel the turnips and slice into ¼-in/0.75-cm rounds. Boil them for 2 minutes, then plunge them into cold water, drain them and set aside.

Heat plenty of vegetable oil in a pan. Dip the vegetables individually into the batter and deep-fry them in batches until they are golden. Sprinkle over a little salt and serve them immediately with the date chutney.

Butternut Squash Dumplings with Sage Butter

These dumplings are very tender and soft, a plate piled with sunset orange spheres specked with the green of the sage. It is a good idea to poach one before cooking them all, to test its consistency. If it disintegrates as it cooks, add a little more flour and test it again. Also you may prefer a firmer dumpling. I like them with as little flour as possible; their fragility comes as a contradiction to the hearty mouthful one is expecting.

If you are cooking the whole of this menu, prepare the dumplings to the reheating stage, in advance of cooking the fritters.

1½ oz/45 g butter	*3 oz/85 g Parmesan, freshly*
3 tablespoons olive oil	*grated*
3 teaspoons sage, finely chopped	*4 oz/115 g flour and extra for*
2 cloves garlic, peeled	*dredging*
1½ lb/675 g squash purée	*salt and black pepper*
(drained weight); made from	
2½ lb/1.1 kg squash (weight	
including skin)	

Place the butter, olive oil, sage and garlic in a small saucepan. Heat it until the butter melts and leave it to infuse.

To make the purée, open the squash and remove the seeds and fibrous matter. Without removing the skin (this becomes much easier when the vegetable is cooked), cut it into sizeable chunks and steam them for 20 minutes or until the flesh is soft. When it is cool enough to handle, scrape the flesh into a food processor and reduce it to a purée. Place it in a sieve standing over a bowl and drain it for ½ an hour. Discard the water and weigh out the desired quantity of drained purée.

Stir in 2 oz/55 g of the Parmesan and the flour. Season with salt.

Have a bowl of flour to hand, drop teaspoonfuls of the mixture into the flour and gently roll them until they are coated. Tease them into spheres and set aside on a floured plate or tray until required.

Bring a large pan of water to an ambling boil and cook the dumplings in batches for 3 minutes; allow them to rise to the surface and give them a minute longer. Remove them with a slotted spoon and place them in a gratin dish. When they are all cooked dribble over the sage butter, discarding the garlic cloves. Sprinkle the remaining 1 oz/30 g of Parmesan over, add a grinding of black pepper, and place the dish in a medium oven until the dumplings are heated through and the Parmesan has melted. If necessary give the dish a few minutes under the grill.

Potatoes, Stilton and Pomegranate Seeds Warmed with Hazelnut Oil on Leaves

This is a delicious combination of tastes and colours. Flashed under a hot grill and served tepid, the flavours are heightened and the textures a touch more yielding. Walnut oil is as good as hazelnut oil here.

Pomegranates are a noble, mysterious fruit, born to adorn. No eighteenth-century Flemish still life of fruit would be complete without a few carefully placed pomegranates. They are to be found as far back as the Old Testament – in the book of Exodus the robe of Euphod was decorated with pomegranates of blue, of purple and of scarlet.

3 oz/85 g small spinach leaves, or enough to cover the base of a platter	*½ pomegranate*
	6 oz/70 g Stilton
	hazelnut oil
14 oz/400 g new potatoes	*salt and pepper*

Wash and dry the spinach well, and reserve it in a bowl. Scrub the potatoes and boil them for 10 minutes. Leave them to become tepid. Scoop the seeds from the pomegranate into a small bowl, carefully removing any white pith. Break the Stilton into small cubes.

Preheat the grill. Toss the spinach leaves in hazelnut oil and season them. Line a platter with them. Break the potatoes into pieces, toss them in hazelnut oil, salt and pepper, and arrange them on the leaves. Scatter over the cubed Stilton. Flash the platter under the grill for 1-2 minutes until the surface of the Stilton just begins to melt and the exposed leaves wilt. Sprinkle some pomegranate seeds over the plate and serve.

Monte Bianco

The origins of this dessert lie with a mountain in the Alps, Mont Blanc, whose eternal snows it is supposed to resemble. It consists of a mountainous pile of chestnut and chocolate strands, crowned with a cap of sweetened cream. Made in quantity for a party, a large platter piled heavenwards makes a very impressive dessert.

There is no doubt that peeling chestnuts is quite laborious. A sensible labour-saving, particularly for a party, would be to use tinned purée, which is extremely good.

---

1 lb/450 g chestnuts, or ³/4 lb/
   340 g tinned purée
milk
6 oz/170 g bitter chocolate

2 tablespoons dark rum
³/4 pint/450 ml double cream
1 heaped dessertspoon icing sugar

Make a horizontal slash in each chestnut. Boil them for 30 minutes. Cool them in cold water and peel them, removing as much of the inner skin as possible. Return them to the pan and cover them with milk. Cook them for 15 minutes or until they absorb the milk. Pass them through a sieve or mouli-légumes.

Melt the chocolate and incorporate it into the chestnut purée. Stir in the rum. Chill the mixture for 1 hour, until it has firmed enough to produce the necessary strands when it is put through the mouli.

Attach the large-hole disc to the mouli and pass the chestnut mixture through it on to a plate so that it forms a mountain peak of strands.

Softly whip the cream with the icing sugar until it starts to peak but is not stiff. Spoon it over the mountain. The dessert can be chilled like this until it is required. Since it cannot be covered, however, do not leave it too long in the fridge or it will acquire other food odours. A cool larder might be a better place for it.

Mince Pies with Apple

(makes 24)

Dried figs make up the bulk of this mincemeat, and with the addition of pine-nuts and marsala it has an Italian echo. The figs should be the moist dried variety; the packet instructions may say that there is no need to soak them. If they are hard and dry, either soak them in water for a few hours or cook until they soften.

While vegetarian mince pies are quite readily available, they tend to arrive along with the wholemeal pastry. A good sweet shortcrust or puff pastry is essential. As a dessert, mincemeat can be layered with double layers of filo pastry and served in squares.

Pastry

1 lb/450 g plain flour	4 small egg yolks
6 oz/170 g caster sugar	2 teaspoons brandy
8 oz/225 g unsalted butter	orange juice

Mincemeat

8 oz/225 g dried figs	1/4 teaspoon nutmeg
1 1/2 oz/45 g raisins	knife tip of ground cloves
1 oz/30 g almonds, blanched	zest of 1/2 orange
2 pieces stem ginger	juice 1 small lemon
1 oz/30 g pine-nuts	2 tablespoons marsala
2 hard-fleshed apples, grated	1 tablespoon brandy
2 oz/55 g shredded vegetable suet	1 tablespoon soft brown sugar
1/4 teaspoon cinnamon	pinch salt

Brandy Butter

6 oz/170 g butter	5-6 tablespoons brandy
6 oz/170 g icing sugar	

To make the pastry, place the flour, sugar and butter together in the bowl of a food processor and process the mixture to a crumblike consistency. Add the egg yolks and the brandy, then add sufficient orange juice to bring the dough together. Wrap in cling-film and refrigerate for 1 hour.

Finely chop the figs, raisins, almonds and ginger, and combine with all the other ingredients for the mincemeat in a bowl.

Roll out the pastry on a floured surface. Using a pastry cutter, cut circles to fit individual cake tins. Allow about ¼ in/0.75 cm for shrinkage and cut the lower circle marginally bigger than the upper circle. Fill each pie with a heaped teaspoon of mincemeat, and cover with the upper pastry circles. Press the edges, paint each one with milk, and bake them for 15 minutes at 170°C/325°F/Gas 3. When they are cool, dust them with icing sugar.

To make the brandy butter, beat the butter and icing sugar together until pale and fluffy. Gradually add the brandy, being guided by taste; take care that it does not curdle.

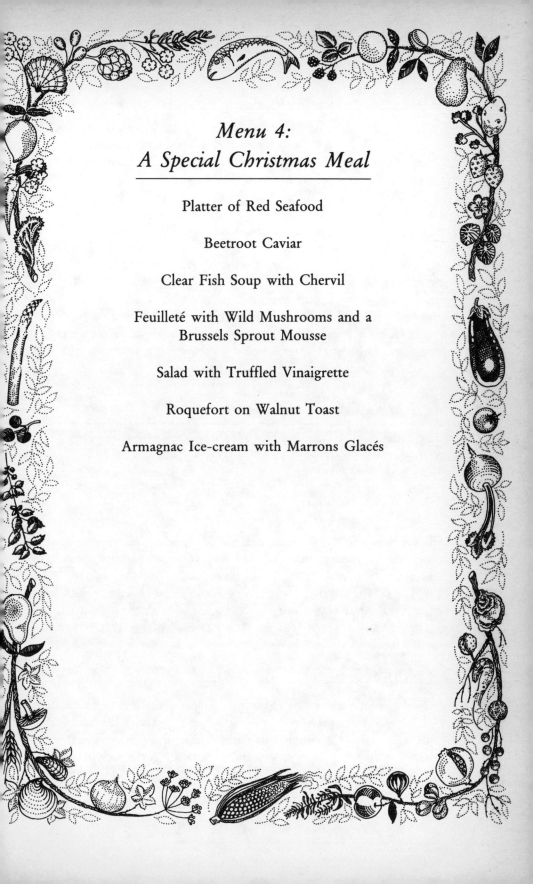

Menu 4:
A Special Christmas Meal

Platter of Red Seafood

Beetroot Caviar

Clear Fish Soup with Chervil

Feuilleté with Wild Mushrooms and a
Brussels Sprout Mousse

Salad with Truffled Vinaigrette

Roquefort on Walnut Toast

Armagnac Ice-cream with Marrons Glacés

Platter of Red Seafood

This dish is simply, as its title suggests, an arrangement of various red seafoods. Take your pick from red mullet, crawfish, crayfish, lobster, gurnard, red bream and any exotica you chance upon. Gut, clean and grill the mullet, gurnard or bream. Halve the lobster by making an incision at the cross below the head and splitting it lengthwise. Remove the grit pouch at the head end and the vein-like dark gut which runs just below the surface of the abdomen. Remove and crack the claws. Should you have a 'hen' lobster, pound the coral and work it into the mayonnaise. The preparation of the seafood is really common sense, it should be presented as 'whole' as possible to achieve the full effect of a mass of coral-red seafood, but it must be prepared to a stage where it does not demand such *coup de force* tackling it as to baffle or embarrass the diner. Arrange the seafood on a large platter, scattered with seaweed, and accompany it with a bowl of garlic mayonnaise and the beetroot caviar.

Garlic Mayonnaise

3 egg yolks	14 fl oz/400 ml pure olive oil (e.g.
1/2 teaspoon mustard	Plagniol) or 7 fl oz/200 ml
squeeze of lemon juice	arachide (groundnut) oil plus 7
	fl oz/200 ml extra virgin olive
	oil
	1/2 clove garlic
	salt

Whisk the egg yolks, mustard and lemon juice together. Slowly whisk in the oils until the egg yolks are saturated and the sauce is too thick. Thin it slightly with water. Crush the garlic to a paste with 1/4 teaspoon of salt, using the flat edge of a knife. Stir this into the mayonnaise and leave it to stand for a couple of hours.

Beetroot Caviar

Beetroot caviar is a mass of glistening, garnet-like dices of beetroot which have been sweated in butter with sugar and with the addition of balsamic vinegar to enhance its natural flavour. A festive crimson, it marries well with the seafood and a bowl of garlic mayonnaise.

12 oz/340 g cooked beetroot	*1 teaspoon balsamic vinegar*
1¼ oz/40 g butter	*1 tablespoon flat-leaf parsley,*
1 level teaspoon sugar	*finely chopped*
salt and pepper	

Minutely dice the beetroot (this can be done in a food processor). Melt the butter and sweat the beetroot with the sugar, salt and pepper for 5 minutes. Stir in the balsamic vinegar and cool the caviar to room temperature. Stir in the flat-leaf parsley.

Clear Fish Soup with Chervil

Until quite recently any decent classical menu would begin with a soup, either clear or thick. Clear soups might be made from meat, poultry, fish, game, turtle or shellfish; they were usually clarified and were often thickened with tapioca. The soup was the entrance to the meal, and to an extent its quality foreran the quality you might expect of the meal as a whole.

Different garnishes come into play such as quenelles of forcemeat, threads of egg, different pastas, little pancakes, croûtons, profiteroles, royales and a chiffonade or pluche. A lengthy list of romantically inspired consommés reads like a roll-call of operatic leads: Alexandra, Bouquetière, Carmen, Célestine, Cendrillon, Divette, Flavigny, Gladiateur, Judic, Kléber, Lucullus, Mikado, Montespan, Nana, Orloff, Otello, Otero, Pompadour, Rabelais and Zola. Most exotic of all perhaps is Consommé aux Paillettes d'Or, a cold chicken consommé flavoured with brandy, poured into cups and scattered with flakes of gold leaf. Perfect Christmas fodder. This takes us into the realm of the 'special' consommés, soups in a class apart regarding qualifying features. To be served in consommé cups, they should be perfectly clear, perfectly delicate, the consistency of a barely setting jelly if cold, and it is no mean feat to achieve this perfect consistency.

In a perfect culinary world a clear fish soup should be prepared as follows: to make 3½ pints/2 litres, acquire 1 lb/450 g of pike, ½ lb/225 g of carp, ½ lb/225 g of tench, ½ lb/225 g of sole trimmings and ¾ lb/340 g of turbot heads. You will also need 5 oz/140 g of sliced onions, 1 oz/30 g of parsley stalks, 3 oz/85 g of leek, 1 small piece of celery and 1 bayleaf. Place these together in a pan with 3 pints/1.7 litres of water and ½ pint/300 ml of white wine. Simmer the stock gently for 40-45 minutes, skimming it occasionally. Strain and season with salt.

To clarify the soup, take 1½ lb/675 g of pike flesh and 2 egg whites, pound them together and place them in a pan. Add 2 oz/55 g of chopped leek, 2 oz/55 g of parsley stalks, and half a bottle of white wine. Mix them well together, add the fish stock and simmer for 30 minutes. Pass the soup through a muslin cloth.

Since pike, carp and tench are not regular guests on the fishmonger's slab, it is necessary to use what is on offer. Sole trimmings are good if available. The soup should be served perfectly hot, in hot bowls, with a 'pluche' of chervil added at the last minute − that is, a frond of chervil without the central stalk.

Feuilleté with Wild Mushrooms and a Brussels Sprout Mousse

This recipe is for all those who hate Brussels sprouts. It is a very pleasant way of preparing the vegetable that is so often an annual nightmare.

Use a selection of wild mushrooms if possible. Otherwise use cultivated mushrooms together with dried wild mushrooms, ideally some morels.

Mousse

2 lb/0.9 kg Brussels sprouts	2 tablespoons crème fraîche
2 scant teaspoons red wine vinegar	salt and pepper

Feuilleté

½ lb/225 g puff pastry	½ oz/15 g butter
1 egg yolk	5 tablespoons white wine
1 lb/450 g wild mushrooms	4 tablespoons crème fraîche
6 spring onions	

Prepare the Brussels sprouts and boil them for 15-20 minutes. Purée them in a food processor with the vinegar, *crème fraîche*, salt and pepper.

Roll the pastry ⅛ in/0.5 cm thick and cut it into rectangles 2 × 4 in/5 × 10 cm. Score diamonds on each one, add a few drops of water to the egg yolk, and paint them. Bake them for 10-15 minutes at 180°C/350°F/Gas 4.

Slice or tear the mushrooms if necessary, and cut the spring onions into thin strips. Melt a small knob of the butter, cook the onions for 2 minutes, and reserve them. Melt some more butter and cook the mushrooms in two lots until they start to exude their juices, or for 2-3 minutes. Return all the mushrooms to the pan, add the wine, cover the pan and cook them for 5 minutes. Remove the mushrooms, add the *crème fraîche* to the pan juices, reduce the sauce by a third and season it. Return the mushrooms to the pan and stir in the onions. Reheat if necessary.

Divide the mushrooms between six heated plates. Place two quenelles of the Brussels sprout mousse in the centre of each plate, discard the bottom of each pastry and place the top half over the mousse.

Salad with Truffled Vinaigrette

'Sexy, rank, foxy, sweaty, scrotal, musty and elusive' is Jeremy Round's commendable attempt to describe the scent of the black truffle in *The Independent Cook*. Sometimes containing a substance resembling the male pig's sex hormone, truffles were once sought with the assistance of female pigs; today the task is normally fulfilled by trained dogs.

The black Périgord truffle, required in this recipe, has partially responded to attempts to cultivate it, and while it is not common, it is available for those sufficiently in love to seek it out. Black truffles were once quite common in the British Isles, less so now, but the Périgord truffles have the edge over their British counterparts in terms of aroma. Unlike white truffles, black truffles can be eaten as a substance, and they will lose some of their quality when preserved in any fashion. Truffle-flavoured olive oil can be used in association with the real thing to extend its presence. Pure essence is a desirable commodity, unlikely to be found for sale in this country.

The white Alba truffle, exclusive to Piedmont, defies any attempts to assist its cultivation. It is prohibitively expensive, and is good for only a week after it has been dug from the ground, so indulge if it ever crops up on a restaurant menu. The white truffle is shaved over food to impart its scent and flavour; it is not consumed as a substance and would be bitter if it were. It does not improve with cooking, either. My first encounter with a white truffle was at the Neal Street Restaurant when Signor Carluccio, the proprietor, produced a tightly closed plastic sweet jar, a quarter filled with objects wrapped in multi-coloured Kleenex tissues. Tissues unwrapped, I was handed a knobbly pale brown tuber weighing about 3 oz/85 g which bore similarities in appearance to a Jerusalem artichoke. The aroma was totally pure, clear and very pungent, like breathing something more than just air. My only disappointment was the packaging — I had expected an inlaid box of rare and exotic hardwood to be produced, filled with the precious tubers sheathed in layers of thin white silk.

Vinaigrette

½ walnut-sized truffle	8 dessertspoons arachide
1 dessertspoon sherry vinegar	(groundnut) oil
½ teaspoon mustard	truffle oil
salt	

Salad

4 oz/115 g mâche	½ walnut-sized truffle
8 oz/225 g broccoli	

To prepare the vinaigrette, first minutely dice the truffle. Whisk the vinegar, mustard and salt together until the salt dissolves. Add the truffle and whisk in the oil. Add truffle oil to taste.

Twist the root from each mâche plant and wash the leaves; dry them between tea-towels or clean kitchen cloths. Set aside in a bowl.

Cut the broccoli into small florets and steam them for 2-3 minutes. Allow them to cool and mix them in with the mâche.

Dress the salad leaves and broccoli with the vinaigrette. Slice the remaining truffle into paper-thin slivers and drop them here and there on the salad.

Roquefort on Walnut Toast

These are intended as little savouries, partly to replace the cheese course. They could just as well be served after the dessert, or as a cocktail appetizer on another occasion. Walnut bread is ideal; failing this, use a nutty, granary bread and serve a few freshly shelled walnuts to the side.

Thinly cut some wide 'soldiers' of day-old bread. Butter them on both sides and place a couple of slices of Roquefort in the centre of each one. Bake them on a tray in a hot oven until the outside of the toast is golden and crisp and the Roquefort is starting to colour. Sprinkle over a dusting of cayenne pepper and serve.

Armagnac Ice-cream with Marrons Glacés

This is a recipe from Nico Ladenis's *My Gastronomy*. It is a parfait, so it does not require an ice-cream maker. It is without doubt the most seductive ice-cream I have ever tasted. Be sure to use a good armagnac, an average brandy will taste like just that.

7 oz/200 g sugar	10 oz/285 g chestnut purée
1 vanilla pod, slit	icing sugar
9 egg yolks	vanilla essence
¾ pint/450 ml double cream	6 whole marrons glacés
3 fl oz/85 ml armagnac	

Make a thickish syrup with the sugar, ½ pint/300 ml of water and the vanilla pod.

Place the egg yolks in the bowl of a food processor and trickle in the hot syrup very slowly at a high speed. The mixture should swell to a thick, pale cream. Continue to whisk until it is cool.

Whisk the cream with the armagnac until it makes soft peaks without being stiff.

Combine the two mixtures and pour into six plastic cups. Cover each one and freeze them overnight.

Sweeten the chestnut purée to taste with the icing sugar and add a few drops of vanilla essence.

Unmould the ice-cream, place a marron glacé on top of each one, and serve it with quenelles or a scoop of the chestnut purée.

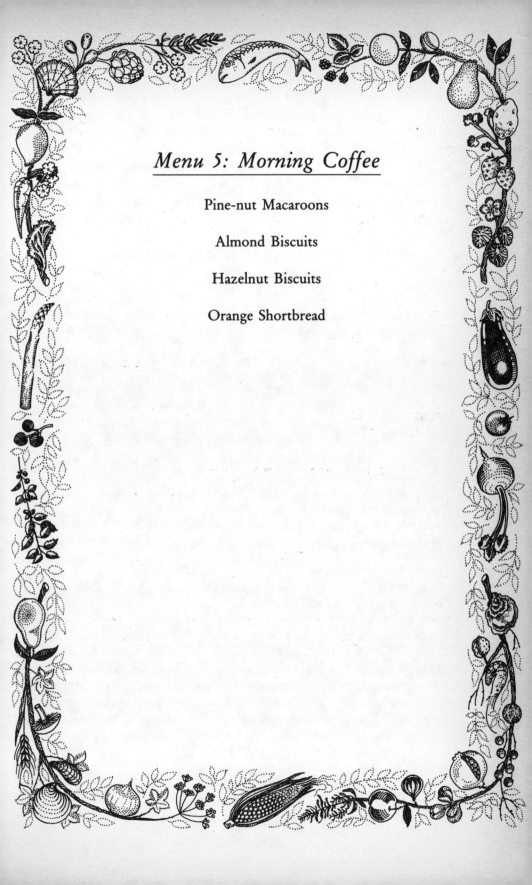

Menu 5: Morning Coffee

Pine-nut Macaroons

Almond Biscuits

Hazelnut Biscuits

Orange Shortbread

Come mid-morning, I develop an unhealthy craving for sugar and white flour, particularly in the absence of breakfast. As we approach the 21st century, food takes on new significance as the government increasingly involves itself in our national diet. This is all to the good, though to adhere to their minimum recommendation of 'nil' sugar would involve a monastic abstinence for even the occasional sweet tooth. I think Egon Ronay's approach to 'eat a balanced diet and leave the rest to nature' is by far the most reasonable approach.

I try to have home-made biscuits on hand whenever possible. These biscuits and macaroons are suitable for morning coffee, afternoon tea, or to accompany desserts, and disappear with alacrity at almost any time of the day.

Pine-nut Macaroons

(makes 20-30)

These macaroons should have a chewy exterior. Too much ground almonds and they will be dry to eat, too little and they will spread too much on cooking. It is worth testing them by just cooking a couple to begin with and adjusting the egg white or almonds if necessary. The pine-nuts can be omitted to produce plain macaroons if desired.

Bitter almonds are not totally essential but they give the macaroons an added 'almond' dimension. You may find them in an oriental or Italian delicatessen, or a healthfood shop.

The macaroons are best consumed within 24 hours.

½ oz/15 g bitter almonds, ground	*2 egg whites*
6 oz/170 g ground almonds	*pine-nuts*
4½ oz/15 g caster sugar	

Preheat the oven to 190°C/375°F/Gas 5. Work the almonds, sugar and egg whites into a paste in a bowl. Form the paste into balls the size of a walnut, using your palms, and roll them in the pine-nuts, pressing them firmly into the dough. Place the macaroons well apart on a baking sheet lined with parchment. Bake them for 15 minutes, then turn the oven down to 150°C/300°F/Gas 2 and cook for another 5-10 minutes. Let them cool.

Almond Biscuits

(makes approximately 40 biscuits)

4 oz/115 g butter	*3 oz/85 g plain flour*
7 oz/200 g caster sugar	*1 teaspoon baking powder*
1 egg	*pinch salt*
vanilla essence	*1½ oz/45 g flaked almonds,*
3½ oz/100 g ground almonds	*toasted and chopped*

Cream together the butter and sugar, beat in the egg and a few drops of vanilla essence. Incorporate the ground almonds, flour, baking powder and salt. Stir in the toasted flaked almonds. Place the mixture in a bowl, cover it with cling-film and rest it in the fridge overnight.

Preheat the oven to 200°C/400°F/Gas 6. Line several large baking sheets with parchment. Using the palms of your hands, form the dough into balls the size of a walnut. Place them well apart on the baking sheets and bake them for 12 minutes. If necessary switch the trays around half-way through.

Cool the biscuits on a wire rack and store them in an airtight container.

Hazelnut Biscuits

(makes approximately 40 biscuits)

4 oz/115 g butter	*5 oz/140 g plain flour*
7 oz/200 g caster sugar	*1 teaspoon baking powder*
1 egg	*pinch salt*
vanilla essence	*1½ oz/45 g toasted hazelnuts,*
3 oz/85 g roasted hazelnuts,	*chopped*
ground	

Cream together the butter and sugar. Beat in the egg and a few drops of vanilla essence. Incorporate the ground hazelnuts, flour, baking powder and salt. Stir in the chopped toasted hazelnuts. Place the mixture in a bowl, cover it with cling-film and rest it in the fridge overnight.

Preheat the oven to 200°C/400°F/Gas 6. Line several large baking sheets with parchment. Using the palms of your hands, form the dough into balls the size of a walnut. Place them well apart on the baking sheets and bake them for 12 minutes. If necessary switch the trays around half-way through.

Cool them on a wire rack and store them in an airtight container.

Orange Shortbread

After several attempts to make a good shortbread I turned to a friend with Scottish ancestry, Clarissa Dickson-Wright, who along-side Heidi Lascelles mans the well-stocked shelves of Books for Cooks. Clarissa agreed that shortbread was no easy item, at worst tasting like a 'bit of old pavement', and provided me with this excellent recipe, the best I have tasted. I have embellished the recipe just slightly; it also makes a good plain shortbread omitting the orange zest.

---

8 oz/225 g butter	4 oz/115 g ground almonds
2½ oz/70 g caster sugar	finely grated zest of 3 oranges
2 tablespoons vanilla sugar	caster sugar for dusting
7 oz/200 g plain flour	

Put all the ingredients into a food processor and process to a dough. Wrap the dough in cling-film and rest it in the fridge overnight. Roll it to a thickness of ⅓ in/1 cm and cut it into the desired shapes. Rest the biscuits for an hour in the fridge; they can be stacked between layers of parchment.

Preheat the oven to 140°C/275°F/Gas 1. Place the biscuits on a lightly oiled baking sheet and cook them for 40 minutes; they should be starting to turn golden when they are removed. Dust them with caster sugar. Allow them to cool on a wire rack and store them in an airtight container.

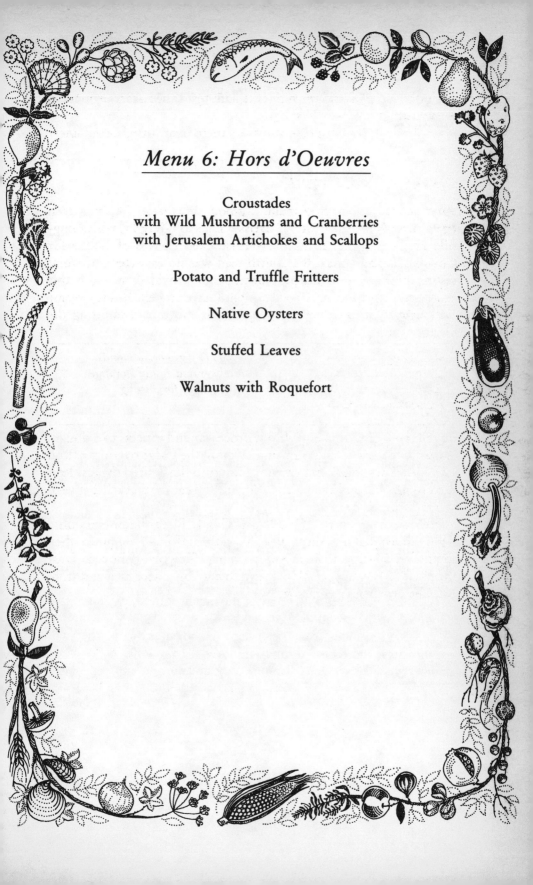

Menu 6: Hors d'Oeuvres

Croustades
with Wild Mushrooms and Cranberries
with Jerusalem Artichokes and Scallops

Potato and Truffle Fritters

Native Oysters

Stuffed Leaves

Walnuts with Roquefort

Croustades with Wild Mushrooms and Cranberries

(makes 20)

1 loaf white bread, thinly sliced	3 oz/85 g butter, melted

Cranberry sauce

3 oz/85 g cranberries
3 dessertspoons sugar

Filling

12 oz/340 g wild mushrooms	salt and pepper
6 tablespoons double cream	

Cut 3-in/1.5-cm circles of bread, paint each side sparingly with melted butter and press them into a tray for individual cakes or buns. Weight it with another tray and bake the cases for 5 minutes in a hot oven. Remove the upper tray and give the cases another 5-10 minutes until they are crisp and brown.

Place the cranberries and sugar in a small saucepan with 3 dessertspoons of water and simmer over a low heat until you have a thick sauce.

Wipe and cut up or tear the mushrooms. Place them in a small pan with the cream. Cover the pan tightly and cook them over the lowest heat for 10 minutes, stirring them after 5 minutes. Remove the mushrooms to a bowl and reduce the sauce by a third, or until it thickens. Season it, and stir in the mushrooms.

Fill the bread cases with some of the mushroom filling and a small spoonful of the cranberry sauce.

These croustades can be filled in advance with the wild mushrooms, and reheated for 10 minutes at 150°C/300°F/Gas 2, the cranberry sauce spooned in once they are hot.

Croustades with Jerusalem Artichokes and Scallops

(makes 20)

There is no denying that these croustades are rich, but in small quantities this is excusable. They should be eaten hot, but are still good tepid.

Try to buy scallops in the shell. If they have been shucked they may have fallen prey to an unscrupulous merchant and been soaked in water in order to increase their body weight. Soaked and then glazed to protect them from freezer-burn, frozen scallops can consist of up to 35 per cent water. Scottish scallops, dived for, are rare and more expensive, but promise a pure and milky flesh compared to the muddy specimens dredged from the seabed. The dredger often shaves the entire seabed, collecting scallops, sand and small stones; this kills the scallops, since they choke on the sand, and does little for the seabed. Diving for scallops leaves the seabed intact. The smaller Queen scallops are ideal for these croustades.

1 loaf white bread, thinly sliced	*3 oz/85 g butter, melted*

Filling

12 oz/340 g Jerusalem artichokes	*1½ oz/45 g butter*
5 fl oz/150 ml double cream	*2 oz/55 g young spinach leaves*
2 tablespoons reduced fish stock	*7 scallops*
salt and pepper	*lemon juice*

Make the croustades as in the previous recipe.

Preheat the oven to 180°C/350°F/Gas 4. Peel the Jerusalem artichokes, placing them in a bowl of acidulated water as you work. Finely slice them and arrange the slices in a small gratin dish. Mix the cream and fish stock together and season it lightly with salt and pepper. Pour this over the artichokes, cover the dish and cook them in the oven for 25-30 minutes. They should be coated in a rich, thick sauce when they are cooked.

Make a *beurre noisette* with the butter. Melt it over a low heat, skim it and decant the clear yellow liquid to a bowl, leaving the milky residue in the pan. Wash the pan out and return the clarified butter to it. Cook this gently until it turns a dark nutty brown.

Wash and dry the spinach leaves and cut them into strips. Heat a little of the *beurre noisette* in a frying-pan and cook the leaves until they wilt. Season them with salt and pepper.

Remove the gristle from the side of each scallop, avoid washing them and scrape with a knife instead. Cut each one into thin circles. Brush the scallops with the remaining *beurre noisette* and season them with salt. Heat a cast-iron frying-pan to smoking hot and lay the scallops on the base of the pan. The exterior should seal and caramelize almost instantly; turn them using a palette knife and cook them momentarily until this side caramelizes also. Squeeze a little lemon juice over them.

To assemble the croustades, place some of the Jerusalem artichokes in the base of each case. Place a little of the spinach and scallops on top.

These croustades can be assembled in advance and reheated for 10 minutes at 150°C/300°F/Gas 2.

Potato and Truffle Fritters

(makes 40)

The size of a small walnut, these fritters have a coating of crisply fried breadcrumbs and a centre of potato purée studded with truffle. There is endless scope for flavouring the purée, and it takes little extra time to put together a selection of fritters, maybe varying the shape to distinguish between the types. They can be coated with breadcrumbs, oats, wheatgerm, sesame seeds or some other ingredient that fires your imagination, although breadcrumbs are preferable for the truffle purée.

They can be deep- or shallow-fried, but deep-frying guarantees neat, evenly browned fritters.

1 lb/450 g potatoes	1 heaped tablespoon truffle,
2 egg yolks	finely chopped
salt and pepper	1 egg
truffle oil	breadcrumbs
	oil for frying

Peel and boil the potatoes. Drain them and allow the surface moisture to evaporate. Alternatively they can be steamed. Pass them through a sieve or mouli-légumes. Bind the purée with the egg yolks, season it with salt, pepper and truffle oil and stir in the chopped truffle.

Form the purée into balls the size of a large cherry. Dip each one in egg and roll it in breadcrumbs. Heat plenty of oil and deep-fry them until they are golden.

Native Oysters

No amount of marketing is ever likely to assuage the true oyster-lover's passion for native or flat oysters by foisting on him the gastronomically inferior 'Pacific' oyster.

The severe winter of 1963, apart from turning lakes and rivers into a Christmas card scene of skaters, sledges and dogs on ice, proved almost fatal to the European or flat oyster (known here as the native oyster), wiping out 80-90 per cent of stocks. The Portuguese oyster, which today is found naturally only in Portugal where it originates, was introduced to France and to a small extent to this country during the 1960s. By the end of the 1960s many were diseased and dying, and attention turned to the Pacific oyster, which originated in Japan. This oyster now accounts for some 90 per cent of the trade. A further, almost fatal blow was dealt to the European or native oyster during the years 1977-82, when a parasite native to California, *bonamia*, was wittingly or otherwise introduced to Europe, wiping out some 80-90 per cent of these oysters in Northern Europe. The parasite is harmless to humans and small pockets of oysters have remained resistant to the disease, although all that remain are potentially infected. This disease has left Pacific oysters unscathed.

All this goes to make native oysters a rare and expensive treat, but worthy if you are inclined that way. Oysters are graded according to their size, ranging from a No. 1 which is the largest through to a No. 4, and, even smaller than that, 'button' oysters. An oyster merchant on the Helford River, who supplied us with a fabulous abundance of native oysters one weekend there, recommends the No. 3 as being the most ladylike mouthful. He believes many women are put off oysters because their first experience of one is a No. 1, which is simply too large. I put this to a London fish supplier, who was sceptical and proposed that any merchant is likely to have an abundance of No. 3 over No. 2 or No. 1, so this sell makes commercial sense. He recommended a No. 2 as the perfect size. As for the 'ladylike' theory, he suggested that if you enjoy something then presumably the bigger the mouthful the better, and perhaps the lady simply did not want it in the first place. All this is assuming that one actually has a choice of size, not so often the case.

Serve them in their shell, on a bed of crushed ice and seaweed, at most interrupting their virgin state with a squeeze of lemon.

Stuffed Leaves

These are miniature parcels of spinach leaves stuffed with saffron risotto (some other risotto could be used, but the saffron yellow looks particularly attractive). Since the risotto should have cooled and firmed before it is used, it is an idea to make it for supper the day beforehand. The leaves are blanched to facilitate stuffing them. Serve them on a base of radicchio leaves.

young spinach leaves	*olive oil*
½ quantity saffron risotto (see p. 84)	*cocktail sticks*

Wash the spinach leaves and remove the stems. Blanch the leaves and dry them on a towel. Place ½ teaspoon of risotto on each leaf, wrap the sides of the leaf inwards and roll each one into a log-shaped parcel, 1 × ½ in/2.5 × 1.25 cm. Secure them with cocktail sticks, concealing the end of each stick inside the parcel.

Just before serving them, lightly brush each parcel with olive oil and heat them for a couple of minutes under the grill. This is not to brown them, but they should be heated through and there should be a change in the texture of the leaf.

Walnuts with Roquefort

(makes 30)

It is comforting to know that efforts to produce the foolproof nutcracker are still under way. Fresh walnut halves are preferable to the preshelled variety in this instance, for those who have mastered the art.

4 oz/115 g *Roquefort*
1 oz/30 g *butter*
Tabasco
lemon juice

3 oz/85 g *walnut halves*
1 oz/30 g *pine-nuts, toasted and*
chopped
cayenne pepper

Place the Roquefort and butter in a bowl with a few drops of Tabasco and a squeeze of lemon juice, and cream them together into a paste.

Spread some of the cheese on each walnut half, dip it into the chopped pine-nuts, and minutely dust with cayenne pepper. Chill until required.

Index